HAUNTED
BRISTOL

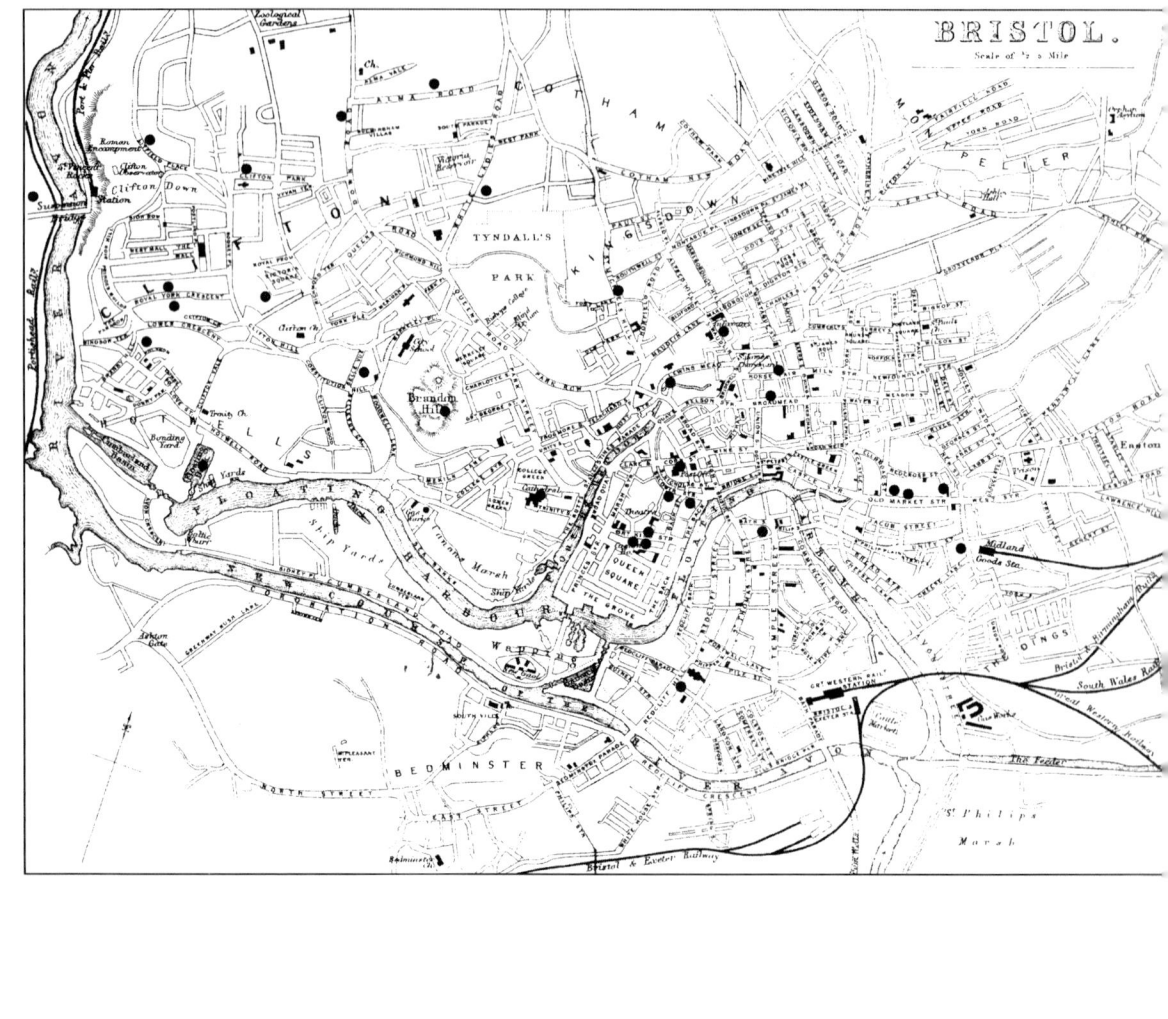

HAUNTED
BRISTOL

SUE LE'QUEUX

Sue Le'Queux

TEMPUS

Frontispiece: *Ghostly hotspots in Bristol. Some of the accounts mentioned in this book fall outside the range of this old map of Bristol however it does offer an idea of ghostly activity within the city limits. And surely there are plenty more that can be added!*

First published 2004

Tempus Publishing Limited

The Mill, Brimscombe Port,
Stroud, Gloucestershire, GL5 2QG
www.tempus-publishing.com

© Sue Le'Queux, 2004

The right of Sue Le'Queux to be identified as the Author
of this work has been asserted in accordance with the
Copyrights, Designs and Patents Act 1988.

British Library Cataloguing in Publication Data.
A catalogue record for this book is available from the British Library.

ISBN 0 7524 3300 8

Typesetting and origination by Tempus Publishing Limited.
Printed in Great Britain.

Contents

FOREWORD

Inspiration for this book came from a website for 'ghosts of the west' on the Bristol Beehive Online Community Network: www.thisisbristol.com/beehive.

The Bristol Beehive is one of twenty-two networks run by Northcliffe Electronic Publishing as part of the Northcliffe Newspaper Group's '*thisis*' news and information website service across the UK. Any non-profit organisation, or individual, can build a free website quickly and easily through Beehive without the need to know traditional web design skills.

This particular ghost site had been created by Beehive staff, and Tempus Publishing approached us to ask if we were interested in turning it into a book. We decided to concentrate on Bristol – the scene of many interesting paranormal experiences over the centuries – and with the help and support of our sister company, the *Bristol Evening Post*, the ghost quest began.

I have tried to include as many hauntings as possible, but Bristol is such a thriving place for the spirit world that some have had to be left out. I have, however, included some ghost stories that still need more questions answering. So if you know more about any of the ghost stories in this book, please let me know. We have created a Beehive website you can visit at: http://beehive.thisisbristol.com/hauntedbristol

While you're there, why not think about creating your own Beehive website. The topic is entirely your choice; you could write about the history of your area, or your own family history – as well as many other subjects. It is also the ideal place to find out what's going on in your community and nationally. There is unlimited free help from the Beehive helpdesk to get you started. Ring 0870 240 3593 or email beehive@nep.co.uk.

I would like this book to encourage people to visit the Beehive Message Board http://www.nepforums.co.uk/beehive and post their stories, questions, thoughts and theories about the ghost world.

I sincerely hope you enjoy this book as much as I have enjoyed researching and writing it. And don't have nightmares!

Acknowledgements

I would like to extend a huge amount of sincere thanks to some very important people, without whom I would not have been able to complete this book: Matilda Pearce and David Buxton at Tempus Publishing Ltd. Everyone at Northcliffe Electronic Publishing; in particular I would like to thank Elaine Pritchard, Project Manager, for giving me this great opportunity, for guidance and for editing the book, and Nathan Corns, Community Development Manager, for imparting technical knowledge and for covering for me while I chased ghosts; Darren Holden and Sally Parkin on the Beehive Helpdesk for invaluable research and help with the images – I couldn't have done it without you; Matthew Bailey – thanks Matt for your help and expertise; Genevra Jones who wrote two of the stories in the book – thanks for all your help with the researching; Stan Szecowka and Gerry Brooke of the *Bristol Evening Post* for allowing us access to your archives and for your good advice and support; Bygone Bristol – for very, very fast and friendly service and for permission to use some black and white photographs; Richard Hope-Hawkins, theatre director, for kind hospitality, sharing of experiences, the lovely print and for making my mum's day – she has discovered Russ Conway all over again! Ken Taylor for the 'Black Castle' contribution. Ken's website can be found at www.wordwrights.co.uk.

John Hughes, for letting me pick his brain on the ghosts of Bristol. John provides ghost walks in Bristol and can be contacted for further information on 07786 353719, or email: fabulous208@hotmail.com.

Arno's Manor Hotel, Sarah in the Llandoger Trow for help with an update on the fourteen ghosts; Bristol Reference Library; Malcolm Farmer for creating a great website on Bristol and providing access to old maps, the web address is www. smilodon.plus.com/mapcd; Old-maps.co.uk – for the same; Olivier Verngault for his input and being brave enough to go ghost hunting; The Bristol Old Vic; and Theatre Royal.

To my family – husband Glyn and daughters Emily and Laura – thank you so much for all your support and understanding while I was absorbed with the ghost quest. And to my mum, Norma Le'Queux, for accompanying me on the ghost quest and a multitude of other help. Finally to my good friend Vanda Wood, thank you for your belief and support.

If I have missed anyone out it is certainly not intentional and please do accept my apologies. I appreciate all the help and advice that everyone has given me and I hope you all enjoy the book.

Introduction

The Dead don't die. They look on and help.
David Herbert Lawrence (1885-1930)

This quotation from D.H. Lawrence reflects my own personal view on the existence of ghosts, spirits and the afterlife. Everyone has some opinion on the subject and I'm certainly not here to influence anyone into believing or disbelieving.

What I have done with this book is to gather together ghostly stories and strange accounts – many of them reported over the years in the *Bristol Evening Post*. In some cases I have added snippets of local history and posed questions which I feel remain to be answered. I hope it may inspire readers to dig a little deeper and investigate the stories further for themselves. Understanding the local history of a place can sometimes help us to understand and discover what the psychic activity is, and possibly why it is there.

What is my own opinion? I can't say for certain that I have definitely seen, or heard, a ghost but I believe that I have felt the presence of one or two. One of my first unusual experiences happened when I was about seven years old. It was the early 1970s and I had been playing in a park with friends near my Staffordshire home. Just next to the park, and over an old cobblestone road, was a row of derelict houses with their windows boarded up. Being a bit mischievous we decided to go and play where we were always being told we couldn't, and went to investigate the houses. One of my friends and I went in through the back gate to the house in the middle of the row. While my friend was distracted by something in the yard, I walked over to the back door, which was open; hanging off its hinges. I could see into the room and immediately in front of me were the stairs to the upper floor.

I had just bent down to pick up a book that was lying on the floor when I heard footsteps on the stairs. I quickly looked up but there was no one there. The sound of the footsteps continued and I felt the air get really heavy. I turned and ran, grabbing my friend on the way out.

A couple of days later I went back to the park and sat on the bench which faced the houses. I could see the house well, but it was far enough away for me to feel safe. It looked different somehow. As I stared I saw what had changed – one of the bedroom windows was no longer boarded up and through the window I could see what looked like a model ship, the really old-fashioned pirate type. It had white sails but looked as though it had red paint splashed over it. I told my friend about it the next day and made her come with me to the park so that I could prove it to her. When we got there, the window was boarded up.

Various things have happened to me since then but probably the most relevant to this book is why I believe 'the dead don't die. They look on and help'.

It seems as though I was destined to work for Northcliffe Electronic Publishing. Some may say it's just coincidence but I think that one or two my ancestors were looking on and helping. A great-great uncle of mine had once worked as a journalist for Alfred Harmsworth, later to become Lord Northcliffe. William Le'Queux was a writer who also worked with Harmsworth when he edited the *Daily Mail*. I began researching Le'Queux's history – which proved quite difficult as he really *was* a man of mystery. There were connections with Jack the Ripper, Rasputin, Crippen, Russia, the Balkans, spies … the list went on and on and, well, that's another story. But that was how I knew of the Northcliffe connection.

Moving forward in time, my father – a huge Frank Sinatra fan – sadly passed away after a long illness in July 2000. I had been brought up listening to 'Old Blue Eyes' so it only seemed fitting that we played Frank's songs at Dad's funeral. Not long after this I became restless in the job I was in. In 2001 I saw an advertisement for a job managing one of Northcliffe's Beehive Online Community Networks. It looked fantastic, and I immediately applied. I hadn't really focused on the name of the company and didn't immediately make the connection with the Northcliffe my ancestor had worked for, particularly as in my research Northcliffe was mainly referred to as Harmsworth. However, I was asked to an interview and then contacted again to go for a second one. I tried really hard to keep from getting overexcited, but I just felt that this was the right job, everything felt just right.

I set out for my second interview, which was to take place at the *Derby Evening Telegraph,* quite early to make sure I was on time. I arrived and made my way to the *DET* building taking a route through the park. It was very early, very cold – being early March – and there were not many people about. A busker was standing by the bridge playing a saxophone and I thought I recognised the tune but just couldn't place it. My interview was the best I'd ever had. It was so comfortable but I still had this inexplicable feeling as though someone was helping me, while the tune I'd heard played by the busker kept going round in my head. And then I was told I had the job. I couldn't believe it. I was really amazed but so pleased.

On the way home the tune I had heard the busker play was still driving me round the twist, as I just couldn't think what it was, only that I had to find out. When I got home I began sticking CDs on the stereo trying to find it. Then it suddenly clicked. It was a Frank Sinatra song but not a familiar one, not one you would immediately associate with him. Certainly not one that had been on constant repeat at our house, but still one I knew. I checked the CD and found it – the tune that I heard was the song *The Girl from Ipenema* and the lyrics that matched the section that had kept going round in my head all day were: *'But I watch her so sadly, How can I tell her I love her?'* I can't explain how hearing a few bars of a tune had left such an impression on me only that at exactly the time I heard it I felt that there was some presence there. I felt as though my dad had made himself known; that he wanted to let me know it would be okay. I honestly believe that he was with me on the day of my interview, helping me to achieve something that would change my life for the better and telling me it was the right path to take. And I also think the 'Master of Mystery', William Le'Queux, may have had a hand in it as well.

So now here I am, writing a book for the very company that my mysterious ancestor worked for and – as an added bonus – working with a fantastic bunch of people as well. They don't call me the Queen of Coincidences for nothing!

That was my story, at least one of them. I have had more experiences like this, which have contributed to the forming of my own particular opinion. But as I said at the beginning everyone has his or her own thoughts.

The more you think about it, though, more questions are raised than answers. If ghosts really do exist why can some people see them, or connect with them, while others cannot? If they don't exist, what is it that people who say they've experienced one see? Is it a chemical or physical reaction? Is it some scientific discovery waiting to be found? Why do some manifestations of ghosts look exactly like people who have lived, yet others are only vapour?

There is a theory that the energy of events and people are soaked up and recorded by the earth and stone in the same way that a video camera records events. These events are then triggered by something and play over and over again. Another theory is that spirits are those who cannot rest, or have some unfinished business in this world.

The television programme *Ripples in Time* broached the theory of time travel, or time collision, as an answer to ghostly sightings. This is not a new theory though, and Carl Jung wrote about his own experience of this in *Memories, Dreams and Reflections*, recounting his strange experience in Ravenna as a moment in which the subconscious and conscious meet. During a trip to Ravenna, Italy, in the 1930s Carl Jung and a travelling companion visited the Neonian baptistery and saw a mosaic in which Christ is shown holding out a hand to Peter who is about to drown. They discussed this at length but on their return to Zurich, while trying to find a photograph of this mosaic, they realised that the image they had seen did not exist. What they had seen was the mosaic as it had been years previously before being damaged and later rebuilt. He described it as when the physical eyes perceive a vision that is not real but nevertheless real in experience.

Other scientists think that the body is just a vessel for the mind. And yet the mind is the 'energy' of a living person. So once the body dies, where does that energy go? Can this energy exist in the atmosphere without a physical presence? Maybe one day scientists will discover the truth behind the paranormal, and ghostly activity will no longer be such a mystery to us. Whatever your own opinion, read on about some of the ghosts of haunted Bristol and see what you think.

Sue Le'Queux
May 2004

CHAPTER ONE

CENTRAL SPOOKS

The Ghost of Bristol Old Vic, King Street

We begin our ghostly quest in King Street at the theatre. Genevra Jones spoke to theatre staff to get an update on this dramatic spirit.

Andrew Stocker, the Old Vic's customer liaison officer, walked slowly through the darkened theatre – empty but for cleaning staff – until he came near the paint shop and a pair of big double doors. Here he paused to let the person walking behind him pass by. But the footsteps he had heard so clearly as he walked along the corridors of the 238-year-old building had stopped. He turned – and there was nothing – but the fast fading scent of a musty perfume. 'The smell was lavender', says Andrew, and he knew by the distinctive perfume that he had been in the presence of the theatre's resident ghost.

When people first started sensing the presence of a woman in a high collared long dark dress, they thought they were encountering the spirit of the famous Victorian actress Sarah Siddons. But Andrew believes the woman who haunts the backstage of the Theatre Royal is Sarah McReady, who managed the theatre almost single-handed for twenty years following the death of her husband William more than 150 years ago. 'Her aura is quite friendly', says Andrew, who admits he was left feeling rather unnerved by his encounter with the redoubtable Mrs McReady.

But she has terrified the life out of more than one young actress as she waited in the wings for her cue to go on stage. In fact Mrs McReady's stern presence was enough in one case to force the actress to join the cast – ahead of schedule. Heather Williams was playing the maid – appropriately enough in Noel Coward's *Blithe Spirit* – when the stage manager saw a figure in black heading towards her. Heather wasn't aware of the figure – but seconds later she felt someone push past her. There was no one there – but she was so scared she went on stage. 'It was easier to face 600

The Theatre Royal in the Victorian era.

people in the auditorium, than to stand with Mrs McReady hovering over your shoulder for company,' explains Andrew.

It must be easy to believe in the supernatural when you work in such an old and complex building, full of long dark corridors, shadowy corners, underground tunnels and secret rooms. The setting couldn't be better if you were designing the set for a haunted house.

Mrs McReady lived and died for the theatre she loved, says Andrew, who has worked for the Old Vic for more than twenty years. She only haunts the old part of the building – the areas which would have been familiar to her in life.

Jane Cooke, a scenic artist who works in the paint shop, first discovered the real Mrs McReady while carrying out research into the history of the theatre. And she seemed, unlike Sarah Siddons who was just a visitor, to be the right person for the part.

Mrs McCready worked in the box office. Then, when the audience was seated, she would run around and operate the props backstage – before standing in the prompt corner, which is where she has often been sensed.

According to Andrew, Jane has also felt the presence of the lonely widow. She was alone backstage once when a lantern started moving of it own accord. Terrified, Jane shouted: 'Mrs McReady is that you?' And the lantern ceased to move.

The figure, dressed in a high-collared black dress, her hair smoothed back from a centre parting and swept into a bun at the back of her head, has been seen in corridors and stairwells, as well as off stage. Her presence has also been felt as a

A later picture of the Theatre Royal on King Street.

moment of sudden inexplicable cold air by many people working in the theatre, who have also reported the smell of lavender perfume.

The scariest story comes from Tony, who worked at the stage door, Andrew remembers. He was responsible for security and patrolled the theatre at night in the company of an Alsatian dog.: 'One summer he was checking the corridor which goes underneath the auditorium. It used to be used by people who needed to get into the pit.

'It was pitch black and Tony just had his torch. Suddenly the dog stopped in the middle of the corridor and refused to move. Then it started to bark. Tony went ice cold from head to foot. He felt a woman's breath on his face and heard a voice whispering "Get out! Get out!" He shone his torch but there was nothing there – nothing but a strong musty smell of lavender. Then the voice started shouting "Get out! Get out!" He didn't hesitate – he fled, taking his dog with him'.

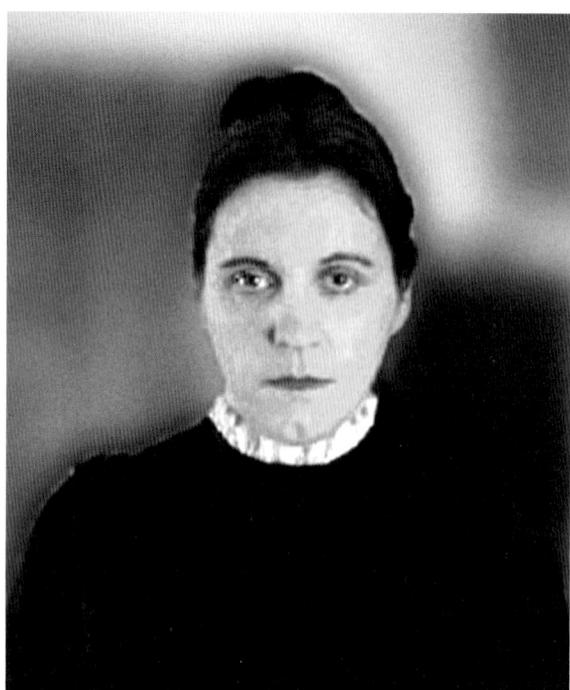

A representation of how Mrs McReady may have looked.

The incident left Tony feeling quite scared. 'He wasn't an easy man to frighten,' says Andrew. 'In fact he was quite a sceptic – until he came face to face with the ghost of the Theatre Royal'.

The ghost of Sarah McReady is not the only spirit to walk the theatre corridors and it seems as though there are at least three. The most active ghost appears in the paint shop where the sets are made. Jane Cooke said she was often aware of a presence beside her. She would see a man in a white shirt and jerkin, sometimes as often as three times a day. Later she found out that a scene painter had died at the end of the nineteenth century when the handle of a huge paint frame, raised and lowered so scenery could be painted, hit him on the temple.

Jane told the *Bristol Evening Post*, in October 1987, that when the new electronically controlled paint frame was installed the machine started moving when no one was near the control button. 'He was obviously dying to have a go,' she said.

Jane thought that his name was Gerald but when Stephen Alexander, a professional clairvoyant, visited the theatre and conducted a séance in the paint shop in 1987, the spirit put this right.

Stephen connected with the spirit and, through automatic writing, it wrote; 'because of the rope I got it'. He was quite possibly suggesting that it was the wire rope, which held up the paint frame, which had broken and caused his death.

The writing however continued: 'My name is not Gerald, it is Richard'.

King William III, King Street

Further up King Street, on the opposite side to the Bristol Old Vic, stands The King William III pub.

In 1998 customers and staff claimed to have heard a spook walking up the back stairs of the historic seventeenth-century listed building and calling out to staff.

Landlord John Thompson told the *Bristol Evening Post* at the time: 'I don't believe in ghosts myself but I can't explain what has been going on. Four of us sat in the bar the other day and it suddenly sounded as if someone was going up the back bar stairs. We all went out the back but there was no one in sight. Other members of staff have also claimed to have heard voices calling their names when there has been no one around. I don't know of any record of ghosts here, but this building has been a pub since the 1660s, so you never know'.

The Llandoger Trow, King Street

At the opposite end of the same spooky street stands one of Bristol's most famous inns, the Llandoger Trow, which is purportedly home to the ghost of a young crippled boy who lived and died in the building.

Strange noises have been heard in the area above the Old Bar. Late at night when the building is quiet it is said that there is an uneasy silence and an eerie atmosphere.

An early photograph of the King William III pub.

*The King William III pub
in 2004.*

The boy's ghost was seen in the mid-1900s by a Mr and Mrs Baker who used to lodge next door to the Trow in rooms that are now part of the inn. The Bakers claimed to have both seen and heard him on the stairs several times. Other people have also heard the sound of his peculiar gait.

It seems, however, that the original ghostly lodger is not the only spirit in residence. A television research team recently sent investigators to the pub and they claimed to pick up the presence of no less than fourteen ghosts.

Built in 1664, the timbered, gable-fronted Llandoger Trow was the real-life inspiration for the pub The Spyglass in Robert Louis Stevenson's *Treasure Island*. The fictional *Hispaniola,* in which Jim Hawkins sailed, is described leaving the quay that is a few yards from the inn. According to a scroll which hangs in the bar, the inn takes its name from Llandoger, a fishing village on the River Wye, and is usually associated with a Captain Hawkins who traded on the Welsh Back in his trow (a flat bottomed sailing barge) and on retirement ran the place. Many famous people have visited the Trow including Daniel Defoe, author of *Robinson Crusoe*.

An early photograph of the Llandoger Trow, with a sailing ship at the quayside.

The Greyhound Hotel, Broadmead

The next ghost is found further up in the city. All that remains of the Greyhound Hotel is the frontage that is now the entrance to the Galleries Shopping Centre – unless the ghost that haunted the hotel for years also stayed on.

No one is quite sure who this ghost is – or even if it is a man or a woman – so it was given the nickname Charlie, but is also known as Mary Lee.

When the hotel was still operating 'Charlie' managed to scare off more than one of the night porters. Bob Collier, who used to be the cellarman at the Greyhound Hotel until his retirement at the age of seventy-six, was not such an easy target though. He was quoted in the *Western Daily Press* in 1975 as saying, 'Really I don't believe in ghosts – and yet sometimes I have thought that there was some kind of presence there. Sometimes it goes very cold and it seems there is someone there'.

This is all that is known at present about this particular ghost, although more would like to be known. Perhaps you know something?

The Grey Monk of Bristol Cathedral

Over in the Old City quarter is an example of Bristol's Old City and the location of our next spirit.

The ghost of a grey monk has been seen several times over the years at Bristol's twelfth-century Cathedral. He has been known to make his way over to the library,

THE GREYHOUND
GREYHOUND WALK
LEADING TO
THE GALLERIES
The Tudor Cart
aditional Cooking

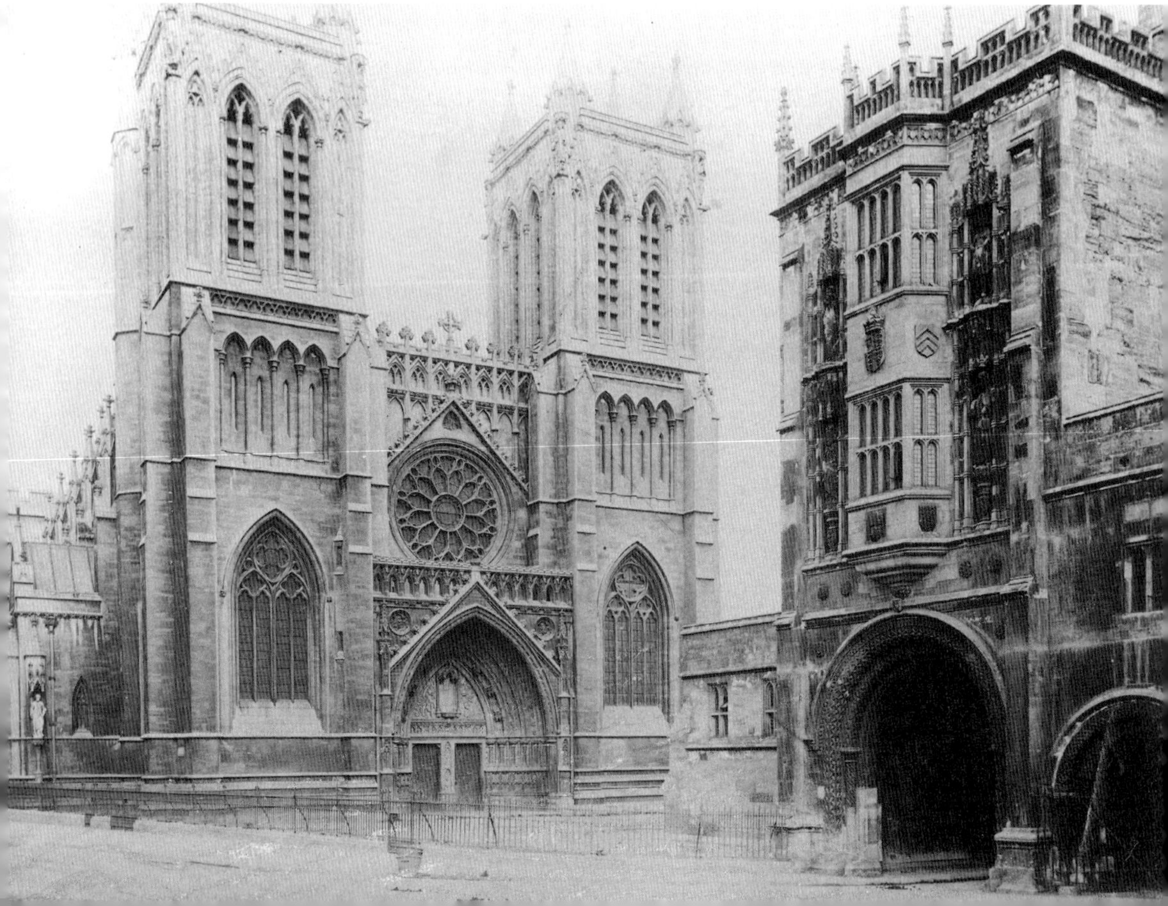

which is next door, and has been seen disappearing through a wall at the side of the building. At this spot you can see the outline of a doorway that has been bricked up.

The Cathedral was originally built in around 1140 when Robert Fitzhardinge founded the Abbey of St Augustine. In 1539 the Abbey was dissolved and the incomplete nave of the building was demolished and built over. It wasn't until 1542 that the remaining portions of the building became the new Cathedral.

The library is built partly on the site of the priory and the grey monk has also been seen here – in the religious books section!

As the habit of the Augustinian monks was black, it is thought that the grey monk, so called because of the colour of his habit, was a visitor to the priory who stayed on.

The Carpetbag Ghost of Redcliffe Hill

Over to the Redcliffe area and the ghost of a woman is said to haunt Phoenix House in Redcliffe Hill, Bristol.

A few years ago a caretaker saw her carrying a large carpetbag. Another man who was working late one night in the building also saw her. He had to go to the top floor of the building and decided to use the lift. When the lift reached the top the doors opened and he saw her on the landing. She was also seen by security guards.

Phoenix House is built on the top of Redcliffe Caves and the supports for the house go right into some of the caverns. Redcliffe Caves have a curious history. There is a story that prisoners from the Napoleonic Wars were kept there. The man-made caves have been hollowed out from the sandstone, which was used in early Bristol glass, and it also seems possible the caves were used in prehistoric times.

The Lamb Inn, West Street

The area of Old Market is where some incredible events happened during the eighteenth century.

The Lamb Inn is the venue for what is probably one of the best-documented accounts of a haunting, which took place between November 1761 and November 1762.

Mr Henry Durbin, a chemist who investigated the phenomena, wrote down a full, contemporary account of the events.

Henry was considered by those who knew him as 'a conscientious, if somewhat pious, and certainly honest gentleman, with a deep rooted Christian faith'. He

Opposite, above: *The frontage of the Greyhound pub as it is today.*

Opposite, below: *Bristol Cathedral early in the twentieth century.*

Redcliffe Hill in the early 1900s.

had no reason to lie about these events and certainly never made any money from telling the story. His story was not even published until after his death in 1799.

This is a shortened version of the events but I would recommend getting hold of the full account as it makes for very interesting reading.

The Lamb Inn was one of the most grand and spacious of Bristol hostels and stood in West Street between Lawford Street and Gloucester Lane. Oliver Cromwell met there with his council of war during his march on Bristol in 1654 and peasants were executed and hanged from its windows for taking part in the Monmouth Rebellion.

The building was demolished in 1910, but in 1761 it was very active with supernatural, poltergeist-like activity.

Richard Giles took over the running of the Lamb in the late 1740s, and also had a carrier business – running wagons to and from London every week. He lived there with his wife and eight children, a couple of servants and the children's nanny when the haunting began. His two daughters – who were the focus of the haunting – were Molly, aged thirteen and Dobby, aged eight.

The first incident took place on the morning of Friday 13 November 1761. Molly and Dobby were in their beds when they were frightened by the loud noise of someone, or something, scratching at the bedroom window.

They hid under the covers, but the scratching then seemed to come from, and around, the head of each bed. Scared, they ran downstairs to the servants. When

Richard Giles went to check the children's bedroom he could neither see nor hear anything out of the ordinary. He just put it down to pigeons scratching on the roof.

No untoward events occurred for a month, but then on 6 December the scratching started again with increased violence and was this time accompanied with the sound of knocking. It continued on a regular daily basis. When Richard decided to see if he could find out what was going on he not only heard the noises but saw a wooden clothing box in the bedroom move up and down, apparently by itself. He saw the sheet covering the box slide off and the box began rocking as if it was being shuffled across the floor. It then tipped over, emptying its contents onto the floor.

The girls were moved into a bedroom in another part of the building – but this didn't help. The haunting continued, but now the girls were also subjected to physical attacks. Both girls were bitten on their necks and arms; crooked pins were stuck into them and ghostly hands clawed at them, while articles of furniture were thrown around their bedroom.

This continued every night and day. Neighbours who were called in to witness the haunting fled in panic. News of the haunting spread around the city, and reached the ears of Henry Durbin who stepped in to try to solve the mystery and spent a night keeping watch in the girls' bedroom. He tried to find logical explanations for the things that happened but found it increasingly difficult. Some of the peculiar events he logged included the following:

- A wine glass floated across the bedroom and crashed into the opposite wall
- Molly's nightcap flew off her head and 'beat a tattoo on her with the skill of a drummer'.
- Furniture was thrown around the room
- Strange voices were heard
- Curtains moved up and down
- Chamber pots whirled around

And, as Henry wrote, 'several other things happened contrary to the course of nature'.

Eight-year-old Dobby even disappeared more than once, and was found being held under the bed by some mysterious force, unable to cry out. She said that 'a woman in a ragged dress, a brown chip hat and great holes in her stockings' had carried her up the stairs.

When some townsfolk went with Henry to keep watch, and saw similar events, they beat on the children's bed and were answered with a loud squealing noise, which they believed was made by some evil spirit.

Henry and the others asked the spirit questions, which were answered by tapping. The spirit apparently informed them that the trouble had been caused by an old witch in Mangotsfield who had been paid by one of Richard Giles' rivals to cast a satanic spell on Giles and his wagons.

This seemed to be confirmed when one of Richard's wagons became stuck on a road near Hanham. Eighteen horses were needed to move it from the 'spell' that had gripped the wheels. The next day the same thing happened to another of his wagons.

The clergy of Bristol also tried to help and met at the pub to perform an exorcism. They too made contact with the spirit by beating on the children's bed but asked questions in different languages. They were amazed when the spirit replied correctly in Latin, Greek and Hebrew.

When the exorcism was over the Revd Richard Symes, of St Werburgh's Church in Corn Street, prayed for the 'two children grievously tormented'. This ghost was going nowhere though and the haunting continued.

Another witness to the activity, a Major Drax, said that the combined strength of himself, his footman and his coachman had been unable to stop the two children being thrown out of bed and levitated by some invisible hand towards the ceiling. He also said he had marked some pins and placed them in a corner of the room but they were thrown back at him.

Even moving Molly from the inn to one of Richard Giles' other properties didn't stop the spirit terrorising her. The spirit just followed her there.

Then Richard Giles himself had an accident while travelling when the harness on his gig snapped and he was thrown into the road. He said that as it happened there was a ghostly woman standing by the side of the road who, when he looked again, had disappeared.

Henry Durbin was then contacted by an old friend, Mr Jennings, who told him that he had been hearing voices threatening to do him harm, as well as mentioning the trouble at the Lamb Inn. The voices had told him that the hold over the girls was diminishing but the grip over the 'old one' was getting stronger.

When Henry visited the Inn on Thursday 13 May 1762, he found Richard Giles critically ill. A doctor was called in the following day but was totally mystified by Richard's illness, which didn't seem to respond to any treatment he could give. Richard's condition did not improve and he died on Sunday 16 May 1762.

Still the haunting continued and Henry carried on his investigations. During one of the communications the spirit told him its name was Malchi. Henry decided to ask an elderly woman from Bedminster, who was known locally as the 'Cunning Woman' or the 'White Witch', about this spirit. She told him that Malchi was the chief of the familiar spirits and knew all languages and thoughts, 'for there are some learned spirits and some ignorant'.

She did, however, tell Henry how to get rid of the spirit. And so, according to the 'Cunning Woman's' instructions the girls' chamber pots were emptied into a pipkin (a type of cooking pot) on the fire where 'beautiful colours came out of it like a rainbow'. And from the end of December 1762 there was no more haunting – not from that ghost anyway.

Henry Durbin's account of the haunting was published under the title *A Narrative of Some Things Extraordinary that Happened to Mr Richard Giles' Children at the 'Lamb Without', Lawfords Gate, Bristol; Supposed to be the Effect of Witchcraft*. The booklet was printed and sold by R. Edwards, Broad Street, in 1800 and was reprinted in 1971 by Bristol bookshop owner Bob Gilbert.

The clue to the origins of these peculiar events may lie in the history of the building itself. The peasants who were executed and hung from the windows would surely be candidates for the restless spirit.

The All Saints Triangle

The following three stories I have nicknamed collectively 'The All Saints Triangle'; because of their proximity to each other. These spirits roam the same small area and make it one of the most psychically saturated locations in Bristol.

The House in Corn Street

In 1846 Mr and Mrs Jones were the tenants of a house situated next door to All Saints Church, which stands on the corner of Corn Street and High Street. They found themselves at the centre of a haunting which was reported in various Bristol newspapers at the time. The ghost was apparently that of a wizened old man who terrified the couple; Mrs Jones felt an urge to jump out of the window while Mr Jones was gripped with fear from a flickering light that appeared on one of the internal walls. Such was his trembling, so the story goes, that his body doubled up like a ball.

It is not certain exactly who the spirit was, but it is more than possible that it could have been the same spirit of the Black Monk that is said to haunt All Saints Church.

All Saints Church

An apparition of a black-cloaked monk has been seen regularly at All Saints Church over the last hundred years. It is believed that the monk watches over some hidden treasure stashed safely away somewhere inside, or near to, the church. He guards it in the spirit world – just as he did in this one.

Corn Street in the early 1900s.

The story began in around 1538 when King Henry VIII decided that the riches of England's churches belonged to him, and sent his men to gather it up. All Saints Church was one of the treasure houses of the West Country at the time and had become rich through gifts donated by pilgrims visiting St Anne's Well. It was also the home of England's first free library, which was kept by monks and lay members of the Guild of Calenderies.

On hearing that other churches were being robbed and relieved of their wealth, the monks of All Saints decided to hide their valuable silver plate. The priest in charge was entrusted with hiding the treasure and he did a very good job, as even to this day it has not been found.

The priests of All Saints did not use the church's riches for their own personal gain and they lived very frugal lives. They slept on straw pallets and used logs for pillows. When King Henry's officers got around to looting All Saints and seized 423 ounces of gold, silver and jewels, the priests are said to have offered no resistance.

The raider's loot contained plenty of treasure; crosses, drinking cups, paxes, candlesticks, dresses, bells and baubles, yet Henry's men were convinced that even more treasure had been hidden. They had heard rumours that one of the monks had disappeared with some treasure, and, just in case it was still in the

A pencil sketch of the Guardian Monk.

All Saints Church today.

church, the king's men returned to ransack the building. They wrecked the church, splitting open pillars and ripping up floors, but they found nothing.

The first report of the Black Monk came some years later, in the sixteenth century, when the vicar of All Saints said he had seen a black-cowled member of the Guild of the Calenderies in the chancel.

David Shelton wrote in *Gloucestershire Life* in 1972: 'This was remarkable, because the Guild had been dispersed years previously by order of the king. And it was all the more remarkable because the sombre figure seemed to glide down the chancel and disappear into a stone wall'.

Over the centuries several frightened vicars said they had seen the ghost, who usually appeared in the parsonage house built into the southwest corner of the church. In 1830, the vicar and his maid said the monk had materialised and beckoned to them before vanishing, again into a bricked-up wall.

The mysterious monk has been seen at various times over the years. During an air raid in 1942 a man in the vestry was startled to see a monk-like figure standing near a wall. And in December 1948 a woman was decorating a Christmas tree inside the church when the monk walked down the aisle.

All Saints Church is no longer open to the public – and although the monk has not been seen recently at the church, the area reportedly continues to exhibit paranormal activity.

A side view of All Saints Church where the monk has also been seen.

The Rummer Pub

The Rummer pub stands to the back of All Saints Church – which can be seen through the small alley that runs just up from the Rummer. The pub is said to be home to a number of ghosts, and over the years at least three different spirits have been seen inside the pub or looking out of one of its windows.

This historic pub stands on the site of a 1241 pilgrim hostelry, the Green Latis, and the Rummer's thirteenth-century cellars were once used a bar. This complex was rebuilt in the mid-1700s by John Wood of Bath. The building next door is believed to be built over a burial ground and in 1965 workmen discovered bones under the cellar floor.

One of the pub's ghosts is said to be that of a young woman dressed in white, who has been seen walking through a glass door in the pub. In the 1970s, Anne, an employee at the pub, said she saw the ghost of a young woman standing on a small landing in front of a glass door opening on to a passage that led to the boardroom.

She described 'a young lady of about eighteen wearing a lovely, full, white old-fashioned dress, frilled all around the bottom, with wide sleeves. It looked a bit like an old-fashioned nightdress'.

The ghost was small, with long black hair. It seemed as though the ghost was looking towards the main staircase, which was to Anne's left, before turning and passing straight through the glass door behind her. The apparition then turned sharply to the left and disappeared. A cleaner who had worked in the pub had also previously seen the 'Woman in White'.

All Saints Lane, where the pub stands, in the early twentieth century.

The Rummer pub in 2004, closed and awaiting new owners.

In the late 1970s cellarman Mike Perry related his encounters with a ghostly man in the cellar. He first saw him one morning in 1973. It was around 10 a.m. and the figure was standing in the doorway of the cellar. He had a dark complexion and short hair and was dressed in shirt and trousers. There was nothing unusual about his ordinary appearance, however there was just something not quite right about him; something just didn't seem real. Mike shouted out and picked up a spanner only to find that the figure had disappeared around the side of the doorway. Unable to believe what he had just seen he searched the cellar thoroughly himself before searching it again with the assistance of the manager. They could find no one.

Around eighteen months later Mike was again working in the cellar of the Rummer. It was 6.30 p.m. and he had gone down to change a barrel. As he made his way deeper into the cellar he felt as though there was someone watching him. As he slowly turned around he realised that his instincts were right – the same man he had seen eighteen months previously stood behind him dressed in exactly the same clothes. Mike decided to get out of the cellar but found he had to push right past the spectre before he could leave.

St James' Parade

A Bristol ghost hunt that made the headlines in the local press in the 1940s concerned a family of five – the Brittons – who were living in a flat at No. 9 St James Parade, off the Horsefair.

Britain's leading investigator of the day, Mr Elliott O'Donnell, was living in Clifton at the time and Mrs Britton, at this point terrified by the haunting, called on him to help.

The padding of footsteps and tapping noises was increasingly disturbing Mrs Britton, who lived in the flat with her husband and three children.

On a Thursday night in June, sometime in the late 1940s, a reporter from the *Bristol Evening Post* joined Mr O'Donnell and other investigators in an all-night vigil at the flat.

Mrs Britton was sitting with a neighbour who lived in the flat below, Mrs Gilbert, in the darkness of her bedroom.

'I sat in the kitchen – the room where disturbances have been noticed in the past,' wrote the reporter. 'The others had taken up various positions in the flat. After two hours of waiting we heard an uncanny tapping. Some minutes had elapsed after the tapping when there were screams. We all rushed to the bedroom where Mrs Britton lay on the floor in a faint. After several minutes she regained consciousness. She said that sometime after the sitting began she felt the atmosphere of the room change "to something horrid and cold".

'"Suddenly," she added, "we heard strange sounds in the room and the walls seemed to quiver. I looked towards the door and saw the horrible face of a woman moving towards my baby, who was lying in the cot by the bed. I remember hurling myself at it"'.

Mrs Britton told the *Post* that one night she had gone into the kitchen and felt like she had been enfolded by 'an icy breath of wind' and something she described as 'unsubstantial' brushed by her.

Four days later, in an attempt to throw more light on the mystery, Mr and Mrs Britton's top floor flat was wired up so that a complete sound recording could be made.

Helping with the recording was a Mrs Vera Llewellyn who remained in the house with Mrs Britton. Mr O'Donnell and the reporter from the *Post* were also present.

'At 2.15 a.m.,' reported the *Post*, 'Mrs Britton suddenly screamed "Baby" and there was the sound of her falling. We all dashed into the room and she lay in a complete faint in front of the fire – one foot was actually in the grate. Miss Llewellyn said that Mrs Britton had stood up, put out her hands, gone completely stiff, cried out, and fallen face-forward on to the floor. When she came round she was emotionally distraught and was crying. She said she had seen the old woman come in and go towards her baby's cot in the corner of the room'.

The Brittons were eventually re-housed after Dr Irving Bell, Bristol's assistant medical officer of health, heard the recordings made at St James' Parade.

The house, which is now a business premises, stands on the ancient site of a Benedictine priory, and St James' church was originally the chapel belonging to the monastery.

The priory was built in 1128 and a former Prior put a curse on Bristol Castle saying that not one stone of it would sit on another if the priory were not there. Sometime in the 1880s a skeleton, said to be the remains of that same Prior, was found under the steps of the building.

It is also said that a tunnel runs from St James' to Oldbury House on Kingsdown. Although there are many legends of tunnels running underneath Bristol, one at least has been found to be true. During the Second World War a bomb landing in the area revealed a tunnel just below the Scotchman and his Pack and another pub, the King David.

Another spooky monk is said to haunt a cellar in Broad Street. In 1800 a verger and his wife claimed to have seen a black-cowled figure that came and went through a wall where there had once been a doorway. Two more people reportedly saw the monk again in 1940.

The Sealed Cellar

Very close to St James' church stands one of Bristol's oldest pubs, The White Hart in Maudlin Street. Built in 1448, it was one of the original 'White Harts' given permission by Richard II to use the name as the animal was his personal emblem.

For the two years that Terry Watson and his wife Valerie were at the pub they had regular visits from a ghost. Mrs Watson named the poltergeist Aloysius, and he only visited the upstairs of the pub. Sometimes the mischievous spirit would start throwing things off their bedroom dressing table in the middle of the night. And one time Mrs Watson watched as a pair of shoes jumped from one spot on the bedroom floor to another and back again.

Mrs Watson told the *Post* at the time, 'Things just leap about; I was once putting some butter on a roll, I left it and it just jumped off the table. It seemed ridiculous at first. I thought I was going crazy'. She went on, 'He comes for about three or four weeks – then disappears for a while. But there is certainly nothing to be frightened of'.

A workman helping with alterations to the pub was left feeling very scared after one incident. He had tried to move a beam in the pub using a 28lb sledgehammer, but just couldn't shift it. When he turned his back, the beam hit him on the back of the head. He hit the beam again with the sledgehammer but it still wouldn't budge. The spirit obviously didn't want this beam moved.

The pub is 300 years old and the poltergeist is thought to be that of a monk or a victim of the plague.

Mr Robert Johnstone Steven, landlord of the pub in the late 1970s, was asked at the time if there had been any activity from the spook. He said that it had all been quiet, but that when he visited the Watson's before he took over from them, a plate had whizzed through the air and had crashed against a wall.

And he also revealed the mystery of the blocked cellar. In the floor behind the bar of the White Hart is a trapdoor which leads down some very steep brick stairs to the cellar. In the mid-1970s the wall sealing the entrance to the cellar was broken down to reveal Victorian furniture and assorted pewter tankards standing on a table. No one knows why the cellar had been blocked off and it seems strange that those responsible were in such a hurry that they did not first remove the furniture and the tankards. The scene was similar to that of the *Marie Celeste*.

The White Hart pub today.

The cellar is large and behind one wall are the graves of the monks of St James' Priory, to whom the inn once belonged.

Mr Steven also told of the ghost of a pot man who used to be seen in another cellar. In the corner of this cellar is a blocked doorway, which at one time opened into a passage leading to St John on the Wall.

In August 1999 Marcus Stapleton took over as landlord of the pub. He told the *Bristol Evening Post* of the spine-chilling welcome he had had from his pub's resident ghost: 'I was in the bar but could hear noises from the part of the pub the ghost is supposed to haunt. I can explain most of the noises in this pub, but not these. But, more worryingly, I saw the outline of a figure in the CCTV monitor'. Undaunted, Marcus joked: 'As long as the fellow behaves himself, he will be made most welcome. Anyway I don't know how to bar spirits!'

Marcus told the *Post* how lights mysteriously switched themselves on in rooms rarely used, and staff refused to spend any time in the back bar, which Mr Stapleton said was much colder than elsewhere. One theory is that the spirit is that of a man killed in the pub during a row with his brother over land. Mr Stapleton added: 'I'm told he gets active and upset when people in the pub start arguing. Other stories say he's happy when there are flowers around. I think that's a myth, but I'll keep my hanging baskets up just in case!'

Regulars claim it was 'George' who has spooked staff at the Lower Maudlin Street pub for years. Although whether this is the same spook that haunted Mr and Mrs Watson twenty years previously one can only guess.

The Odeon Cinema

Mysterious sounds heard in the Odeon cinema, near the Galleries shopping centre, are believed to stem from a violent event that occurred in 1947, when the cinema manager was shot dead during what was first thought to be a robbery. But no money was taken.

John Hughes began running ghost walks in Bristol in May 2004 and the Odeon cinema is just one of the places on his tour. He explains that screen three is where most of the odd activity in the cinema takes place. Numerous noises have been heard including unexplained banging and footsteps emanating from behind the stage.

Spirits At Work, Nelson Street

Olivier Vergnault is a brave soul, for in October 2003 he took part in an investigation of ghostly activity at the Works Nightclub in Nelson Street, Bristol.

Along with Lainie Smyther, a paranormal investigator and dowser, a team from the Bristol Ghost Club and three *Evening Post* readers, Olivier spent the night at the club, which is built over an old burial ground.

It reached the witching hour – the time between midnight and 1 a.m. when, according to experts in paranormal phenomena, the 'holes' between this world and the Other World are more likely to open – the best time to invoke spirits.

Ghost walker John Hughes outside the Odeon cinema.

Olivier Vergnault and fellow ghost hunters at The Works nightclub. (Copyright *Bristol Evening Post*)

Despite the lack of visible activity that night, Olivier shared the uneasiness of the others as they trooped around the club. Olivier and Lainie had made their way to the ladies toilets – one of two areas in the nightclub where the team of investigators felt a growing unease. The whole group of investigators found the ladies' loo area a particularly unsettling place, not only because of the facing mirrors – said to be a way of opening a gateway between worlds – but also because the temperature in this particular room had dropped very low. To make contact with the Other World they held a brief séance and got a surprising result.

Olivier explained what happened in the *Bristol Evening Post* on 31 October 2003: 'The chill is now lingering in the room. The spirit – possibly that of a murdered woman – has attracted our attention.

'The pendulum sways back and forth and I cannot keep my eyes off it. It signals a "yes". The spirit in our presence seems keen to answer our questions. I am transfixed. Several times, until Lainie and I sit down on the floor of the ladies' loo and started communicating with the Other World, I feel a shiver roll down my spine'.

Lainie then sensed the presence of the spirits of two women. One spirit did not want to talk, however the other communicated to them that her jealous husband murdered her with poison. Lainie said that the spirits wanted to be freed, but she didn't have the skills to help them cross over.

Olivier could not see the two spirits, but he did begin to believe that there was some sort of presence and that the beings were indeed answering their questions. He was hoping to witness some of the strange happenings that staff had experienced over the years, which included shadowy figures running along corridors, loud bangs on doors and pint glasses smashing to the floor in the night. Some Works staff had also claimed to have seen the apparition of a child dressed in Victorian clothes.

Then one of the members of the Ghost Club left an electric torch in the attic – only to find it dismantled on his return five minutes later! Adrian Darby, from Fishponds, and a member of the thirty-strong Ghost Club, said at the time: 'This is the spookiest thing we've found. That was very strange – there was no one in the attic when we left'.

CHAPTER TWO

SUSPENDED BELIEF in CLIFTON

The Dwarf Highwayman of Clifton Downs

What a terrifying sight it must have been. A body suspended in an iron cage from a tree, rotting away for all to see.

In the 1700s Jenkins Protheroe, a grotesquely deformed dwarf, had set himself up as a highwayman. He preyed on lone travellers in the area of Clifton Down, begging for money, but robbing them if they did not cough up.

Justice caught up with him in 1783 and on March 31 of that year he was hung at Gallows Acre Lane for killing Evan Daniel, a pig drover. Jenkins' body was left to rot, suspended in an iron cage at the top of Gallows Acre Lane, which was near the top of what is now Pembroke Road, as a warning to others.

Jenkins was the last man to be hanged at the spot, and before long the lane leading to Gallows Acre (otherwise known as Clifton Down) became a no-go area as people claimed Jenkins' ghost climbed down from his iron cage to roam the Downs.

A common theme with most ghostly sightings is the reaction animals have to the presence of spirits. This happened in the case of Mrs Daphne Garland, a dealer in antiques, who related this strange encounter to the *Evening Post* in the 1970s.

One night at around 11 p.m., she was exercising her small black and white dog on the Downs in Clifton. She was about 100 yards from where the gibbet once stood. The night was fine and clear with no wind and no hint of fog. Suddenly, her dog started whimpering. She looked around, and roughly twenty feet from where she stood she saw a spiral of smoke rising from the ground straight up into the air. It was estimated that the spiral could have been up to eight feet high.

She had been watching it for around five minutes, when the spiral suddenly vanished. During this time the dog continued to whimper.

Was this the spirit of Jenkins Protheroe?

The execution of Jenkins Protheroe.

Oldbury House, seen from St Michael's Park.

Oldbury House, Whiteladies Road

Oldbury House is a seventeenth-century building in Whiteladies Road, Clifton, situated a couple of doors down from Bristol's BBC headquarters. During the Second World War, the BBC took over this building as a hostel for twenty-eight of its female employees.

Miss G. Methvea Brownlee, a West Country photographer, had been bombed out of her home in Charlotte Street, and moved into the Oldbury House hostel to look after the girls. Miss Brownlee's bedroom was on the ground floor of the hostel near to the front door. One night she was awakened by thuds, dragging sounds and a child sobbing – and then the ghostly visitations began. Her description of the ghosts appeared in the *Bristol Evening Post* at the time: 'There was a very tall, thin man, dressed rather like a monk in long dark robes, with a bunch of keys hanging from a girdle at his waist,' she said.

'There was also a little old woman, dressed rather like a housekeeper of the same period and finally there were five ladies, always together, dressed alike in clinging robes and high head dresses'.

On further research, Miss Brownlee found out that there had at one time been an opening from her room into the stables.

Oldbury House in 2004.

'It was here I first saw the monk. After that, at frequent intervals, I saw not only the monk but also the housekeeper and the five women together.

'The women seemed to stand on a balcony, as if in a vision. They talked agitatedly amongst themselves, and in the background there was the monk again, pleading for something'.

Miss Brownlee said nothing to the girls in the hostel, because she didn't want to frighten them, but eight of them told her of figures they had seen in the building. The other twenty neither saw nor heard anything.

After three months the haunting had preyed on the nerves of those living there so much that the hostel was subsequently closed.

In 1642 the English Civil War began and King Charles I placed Prince Rupert in charge of his cavalry, which was nicknamed the Cavaliers by Cromwell's Parliament army. Prince Rupert is thought to have used Oldbury House as his headquarters when Cromwell's army besieged Bristol in 1645. It may have been chosen as a result of rumours that underground tunnels ran from the house to the centre of the city and to the old Bristol Fort.

The BBC Ghost

On 24 June 1985, Rebecca Gooch reported in the *Bristol Evening Post* on the return of the BBC studio spook.

The BBC building as it is today.

Two views of Whiteladies Road in Clifton, taken in the 1920s and 1950s.

At the time Alec Reid was the producer of a new BBC Radio 4 series on the paranormal and inexplicable called *Forbidden Knowledge*. When the programme began recording in May 1985 all sorts of mysterious happenings plagued Alec and presenter Bob Couttie. These ranged from repeated, inexplicable technical hitches in the studio, to an iron girder collapsing in the BBC canteen just as Bob walked in.

Tapes speeded up for no apparent reason; an audio assistant's normally reliable motorbike broke down twice after she edited a poltergeist soundtrack; a digital watch went blank during a photo session; machines would break down wherever they were; and strange gaps appeared on recordings.

Alec told Rebecca at the time: 'These events became so frequent that we began keeping a record and we've now worked out that although technical hitches can and do occur all the time, there have been exactly twice the normal number during the time we've been recording'.

Studio two was the biggest problem. It was in the same building as the 'spooky' Studio A, where, in 1975, producer Ann Owen experienced a series of odd events while working on the paranormal television series *Leap in the Dark*.

After interviewing a woman in Bavaria who was hounded by an electronic poltergeist, Ann had returned to Studio A to work on the soundtrack when every piece of electrical equipment in the studio broke down. Not long after that a huge bookcase that was nailed to the wall mysteriously broke loose overnight.

While Ann was editing another episode on mysterious drownings, a glass of water suddenly hurled itself at her script.

Could advances in technology have opened up another portal for the spirit world to be able to communicate with us?

Brunel's Ghost, Leigh Woods

Just over the Clifton Suspension Bridge are Leigh Woods where another famous ghost 'lives'.

The ghost of Isambard Kingdom Brunel is said to haunt the area of Leigh Woods, overlooking the Clifton Suspension Bridge, which he designed in the 1830s. People have reported seeing the distinctive figure of the famous Victorian engineer, who died before the bridge was completed in the 1860s.

Leigh Woods themselves have a somewhat eerie reputation. Once, an old tramp was horrified when asked if he had ever slept in Leigh Woods. Going into the woods in daylight was fine but never at night. He said that there were strange things in the woods and that sometimes, unearthly screams are heard.

Animals are known to react strangely in Leigh Woods. A local man told how his Alsatian dog always behaved oddly in the woods. On one occasion the dog jumped up on to a rock, sat down, lifted his head and howled repeatedly. Elsewhere, the dog behaved perfectly normally.

The edge of Leigh Woods, Clifton, photographed early in the twentieth century.

No. 14 Bellevue, Clifton

There were some strange goings-on at a first-floor flat in Clifton during the 1960s. No. 14 Bellevue was the home of Mr and Mrs Philip Stone who lived there with their two young children and two pet dogs.

Mr Stone told the *Bristol Evening Post* in December 1964: 'The table will give a loud creak as we are watching television at night. It sounds like the sudden crack of old ship's timbers, though the table is normally as solid as a rock.

'Three or four times a week in the small hours just before we go to bed, the dogs will jump up and start barking. They run to the door and when I open it they run downstairs, sniffing as they go. They always seem bewildered because they find nothing'.

The unidentified groans made by the brand new table were very bewildering but these strange events were not just restricted to the first-floor flat.

'When we lived upstairs, things used to fall from the kitchen dresser, although it was quite level, and once we found broken lager glasses,' said Mrs Stone.

The couple said that in 1962 they had been startled by the sound of scratching from the parapet above their window and a friend who was staying with them was convinced that the house was haunted.

'We haven't seen any ghosts as such', said Mrs Stone, 'but I understand a young woman was killed or murdered here long ago. The house was once a girls' seminary and our flat was used as a dancing room where girls were taught deportment. We have often joked about the happenings, but we don't know what to put them down to'.

Regent Street, Clifton

In 1990 Graham Williams opened up his new restaurant, the Chi Chinese Cuisine in Regent Street, Clifton. But by 1991 – out of sheer desperation – he had to call in some help to try to rid the premises of a smelly spirit.

It seemed that this particular phantom was making its presence felt by taking up residence under table seven and producing a foul smell. Mr Williams tried everything to remove this awful stench.

'I cleaned the carpet, turned on the blower and tried the air freshener – but nothing seemed to work,' said Mr Williams at the time.

'The odour was only noticeable around one particular table. If you took a couple of steps backwards, you couldn't smell a thing'.

He eventually called in Philip Steff, a psychic medium, to see if he could shift the deathly pong.

Despite being a sceptic of the paranormal Mr Williams was amazed, and very pleased, when Philip successfully banished the unwanted spirit from the premises.

It is still not known what caused the smell at table seven; however, Mr Williams later discovered that a woman had died in the basement of the building in the 1700s. Was she making her presence known?

CHAPTER THREE

SURROUNDING THE OLD CITY

The Union Ghost, Avonmouth

You may think that a warehouse is an unlikely setting for a haunting. But in 1975 workers at Spillers Flour and Animal Feeds Mill reported seeing a ghostly figure.

The *Evening Post* newspaper report from 19 December 1975 went on to reveal that this particular spirit was very selective about who he wanted to communicate with, and only appeared to Transport and General Workers Union members. The ghostly figure appeared (to the chosen few) on the seventh floor of the mill and it was reported that an icy drop in temperature heralded its appearance. The shop steward for the union at the time, Mr Charles Horton, said: 'Two of my members who claimed to have seen it were in a very abject state'. It had shaken up mill workers so much that one of them wouldn't go back to the seventh floor for several weeks after he had seen it.

Spillers site manager at the time was Mr David Lapraik and he seemed to take it in his stride. He told reporters in 1975 that unless the ghost affected people's work the management of the mill weren't planning to take action.

Shop steward Mr Horton seemed equally pragmatic: 'It seems as though this apparition has got an element of demarcation. It may well be something of a connoisseur because it only appears to T and G members,' he said. 'But clearly it's got to go. If management don't get rid of it, the T and G will. We will not be beaten by a ghost. As far as I know it is not a card-carrying member'.

The warehouse – which is now ADM Milling – stands on the Old Docks area of Avonmouth which is, coincidentally, close to the fire station – mentioned later in this book, and which also has a history of paranormal activity.

A view of Avonmouth from the Docks, taken in the 1930s or '40s.

Aerial view of Avonmouth Docks, taken in the late twentieth century.

The Cloth Mill, Shirehampton

One of Bristol's old cloth mills, which used to lie in a hollow off the Shirehampton Road, has long since been demolished but people still recall some curious stories about it.

One elderly gentleman recalls an event that happened to him when he lived at the mill as a young boy.

He and his brother were sleeping in an upstairs room one night when he suddenly awoke to see an old lady dressed in black standing by his bedside. She gestured to him to follow and he heard her say, 'Come with me; I wish to show you something'.

Scared, he covered his head with his bed sheets and shouted to his father in the next room. His father's only response was to tell him to be quiet and go back to sleep.

When the young boy looked out from under the bedclothes the old lady in black had gone around to the other side of the bed and was trying to wake his brother up. When his brother didn't stir, he saw her turn away and walk sorrowfully through a wall, where at one time there had been a door.

Legend has it that a man hanged himself at the back of the mill, and the building itself has always had a reputation for being haunted. But the identity of the old woman remains unknown.

The Helpful Waiter, Lawrence Weston

Kim Gye was becoming quite desperate. The ghost she was sharing her flat with in Henacre Road showed no sign of leaving, even after a service of blessing carried out by a Roman Catholic Priest.

Kim's plight featured in the *Bristol Evening Post* on 11 August 1990. She claimed to have seen the ghost of a man wearing dark trousers and a white shirt with an old-style bobbed haircut on at least four occasions. 'My little boy would not sleep in one particular bedroom for at least seven months. He said a man was coming to get him,' she said.

Bristol City Council took her complaint so seriously that they referred her case to the special needs panel to look into re-housing her. But Kim was so afraid to go back to the flat that she moved in with her mother, who had six other children, even though this meant that eleven people were sharing a three-bedroom home.

Kim's mum, Shirley Hannon, told the *Bristol Evening Post* that Father O'Regan, a priest from Our Lady of the Rosary, Lawrence Weston, had performed a service of blessing on the house. The City Council confirmed that Father O'Regan had written supporting Kim's case and had expressed serious concern.

Mike Griffiths, a city spokesman at the time, also confirmed that part of Kim's case for re-housing was that her flat was haunted. 'We are taking it seriously,' he said.

'We are taking it as a legitimate problem bearing in mind we have a letter from a man whose moral credence must be impeccable'.

After this report was published, the *Bristol Evening Post* stepped in to help and asked Mr Philip Steff, car park attendant by day and president of Bath Psychic club and ghostbuster by night, to investigate Mrs Gye's haunted claims.

Mr Steff, a medium, arranged to visit the flat and met with Mrs Gye and some of her friends on 24 August 1990 to persuade the spirit to move on. Kim told Mr Steff about the haunting and that on several occasions she had seen a man in his thirties, once even helping to mend her curtain rail! Mr Steff immediately identified the room where the 'curtain pole repair' had taken place, claiming he could feel the presence almost straight away. 'I'm getting a strong tingling sensation – I think this is going to work,' he said.

The *Bristol Evening Post* reported what happened at the meeting in 1990. Kim was nervous, as were her friends, but Philip Steff reassured them. 'I'm not an exorcist. If it were anything evil I wouldn't be here,' he said at the time. 'I want to help a presence that has been trapped on earth because he or she doesn't understand death, I have to encourage them that they are doing no good here and would be happier in the spirit world'.

As the light faded and silence fell over the empty flat things began to feel a little eerie. Kim, Mr Steff and Derek Goodson – the vice-president of Bath Psychic Club – formed the necessary circle. Mr Steff's breathing changed as he began to enter the trance in which his helper – a Prussian army officer – would take the presence into the spiritual dimension.

'He is a young man, dark-haired. He might have been a waiter in a restaurant,' said Mr Steff. 'He's full of vitality. He's not a trapped presence, he's just interested in children'.

Suddenly Mr Steff stood up and began speaking in a thick German accent. 'All right, friend, we can see you. We know you are here, and we know it is because it was not possible for you to have a young family of your own. So you have chosen this family that lived here, to take an interest in them and watch their antics, and to learn what it would have been like to have children of your own'.

Afterwards Mr Steff gave the spook a bit of a ticking off, telling the spirit he would be better off on the other side, then the trance was over.

Before leaving, Mr Steff, who had not met Kim Gye before, asked if she knew someone called Alice. 'Yes, that's my Great Nan,' she replied, wide-eyed. 'Well, she's here helping,' Mr Steff explained.

Philip Steff went on to provide his ghost-busting service again later that year when he was approached to help a couple that lived in council flat in Hartcliffe.

There are conflicting views on whether spirits should be called up or helped. The Roman Catholic Church, while believing in spirits, does not believe in calling them up because of their potential for evil. The Church of England keeps an open mind, admitting that spiritualism may provide comfort for certain people. It prefers, however, to concentrate on the life before rather than the life beyond death.

But spiritualists like Mr Steff believe that some spirits do need assistance and the process can help those left behind.

Stapleton Woods

Imagine. You're in Stapleton Woods enjoying the fresh air and peaceful surroundings when a man approaches from the other direction.

Just another walker, you think to yourself. As he approaches it looks as though he is going to speak to you. But he doesn't slow down, and when he reaches you he just carries on walking – straight through your body!

This strange occurrence has reportedly happened to a number of people over the years in Stapleton Woods, and the experience has left them terrified.

The area is of considerable historic interest as it is the place where Cromwell gathered his troops before laying siege to Bristol.

The Duchess of Beaufort and the Monk, Vassals Park

One of the large parks in Fishponds is on the Oldbury Court Estate and is known locally as Vassals Park. It is believed that the ghost of the Duchess of Beaufort haunts this area.

It is believed that the Duchess died when she was struck by lightning while out riding on Pur Down, and many people claimed over the years to have seen her ghost riding through the park on a phantom horse.

Terry Sullivan was interested in tales of an eerie white figure roaming around Duchess Lake in the grounds of Stoke Park Hospital, which is now Blackberry Hill Hospital. So he and some friends decided to investigate the area to see if they could catch a glimpse of the phantom. One night their vigil paid off when the ghostly Duchess appeared.

Terry, then a lad of eighteen, gave the following account to the *Bristol Evening Post*, which was published on 19 February 1965.

'It was a big white figure of a horse with a woman sitting on it. It was moving in and out of the trees. We kept seeing it at intervals. Then it disappeared,' said Terry. 'We think it must be the ghost of the Duchess after whom the lake is named. She lived in the mansion, which is now the hospital'.

Other spirits are also rumoured to roam the park. Two teenage members of the Oldbury Court youth club were halfway across the footbridge in the park that leads over the River Frome. Suddenly, they saw a cowled figure appear in some sort of cloak with its arms outstretched. They couldn't see its face or feet and it seemed to float in mid-air. The figure got a quarter of the way across the bridge then stopped, turned back and promptly vanished into the wall a few feet from the end of the bridge.

Oldbury Court Estate, where the ghost of the Duchess of Beaufort has been seen.

Some other members of the youth club decided to visit the spot a couple of nights later and claimed to have seen a white light floating near the wall.

Mrs Doreen Powell is another person to have experienced paranormal activity in the area. She visited the park with others soon after the sighting made by the youth club members and claims to have heard monks chanting. Mrs Powell did have some idea as to what this may have been. Old Lady Vassal told her that there was a monk called William who had been bricked up in the wall.

There used to be a stately home on the estate and the story tells of a Catholic monk or priest who was secretly celebrating mass, at a time when it was illegal to do so.

When visitors arrived, his fellow monks hid him away in a secret passage – a priest hole. Unfortunately, it seems that he was forgotten, so the story goes, and he starved to death.

It seems Mrs Powell was susceptible to psychic phenomena. When she was fifteen years old she lived in a large house in Victoria Park Road, Bristol. A puff of what was thought to be pipe smoke used to appear in an upstairs room. One day her sister entered the room and saw an old man sitting in a wicker chair smoking a pipe. Needless to say she got out of there as quickly as possible.

Another house in Victoria Park Road was supposedly built on the site of an old lunatic asylum and was so badly haunted that it was exorcised. After the exorcism, the ghost of a young girl of about ten was seen at the bottom of the stairs. Smiling,

View of the lake in Oldbury Court gardens.

she climbed the stairs and vanished. Nothing supernatural was ever seen in the house again.

The Post Office Tavern, Staple Hill

The Post Office Tavern at Staple Hill, Bristol, was a large rambling pub haunted by footsteps, clicking noises, a powerful smell of perfume and a presence so strong that it once stopped landlady Mrs Mary Kittlety in her tracks.

She and her husband, Bryan, took over the Tavern in January 1976, but it wasn't until the summer of that year that Mrs Kittlety had her first fairly stunning introduction to the supernatural. As she turned a corner in the upstairs corridor of the building she was physically thrown back – 'almost as if I'd hit a wall,' said Mrs Kittlety.

On another occasion she was in the upstairs living room watching television when she heard a man's footsteps outside the door, but thinking it was her husband she didn't take much notice. When the footsteps continued Mrs Kittlety decided to take a look. When she opened the door though there was no one to be seen – yet an overwhelming smell of perfume pervaded the corridor. Mrs Kittlety told the *Evening Post* at the time, 'It went right to the back of my throat; I could really taste it'.

A friend of Mrs Kittlety's had also smelt the perfume, as had Mrs Kittlety's nine-year-old daughter.

One night, Mrs Kittlety went to the bathroom and saw what she described as 'very bright lights' in the passageway and experienced a horrible sensation.

This proved to be the last straw for her and in 1976 she asked her local vicar to pray for the parts of the house where she had felt the presence. She also placed numerous copies of the Bible along the upstairs corridor, which proved to be effective as the strange events immediately ceased. She told the *Post*: 'If anyone offered me £1,000 to take them down, I wouldn't'.

Although the ghost remains unidentified, it is known that a young man had been stabbed to death during a violent fight outside The Post Office Tavern in the early 1970s.

Four Victorian Ghosts, Air Balloon Road

During the early 1990s, Victoria and Stephen Cross moved into No. 157 Air Balloon Road but soon found that they were not alone – they were sharing their Victorian home with four ghosts.

Staple Hill High Street, where the Post Office Tavern used to stand.

A medium was called in and the spirits were identified. One was a boy called Tom; the second a woman in a black dress with a high collar; the third was a teenager called Peter who had died in the house; and the fourth was a man called David.

Victoria spoke to the *Bristol Evening Post* in February 1998 whilst trying to find an explanation for the haunting.

'Old coins from the 1930s turned up in the house for no reason we could understand, and a friend said she saw a vision of a man in one of the upstairs rooms,' said Victoria.

'We had builders in and they could hear footsteps when they were alone in a room, and a puppy we once had used to get very distressed at night in certain rooms in the house. There was definitely something strange going on.

'We haven't had any more trouble since the medium came but I would like an explanation of where the ghosts came from'.

In The Kingswood Area

The Kingswood area, in the parish of St George, includes Hanham and Two-Mile Hill. A description of the parish appeared in the *National Gazette* in 1868:

> *St George, a parish in the hundred of Barton-Regis, county Gloucester, 2 miles E. of Bristol, its post town. It is situated on the river Avon, and includes the hamlets of Upper and Lower Easton, Two-Mile Hill, and Whitehall. The people are mostly employed in the coalmines and quarries. Here are extensive market gardens. The living is a vicarage in the diocese of Gloucester and Bristol, value £530. The church is a stone edifice dedicated to St. George. There is also the district church of St. Michael's at Two-Mile Hill, the living of which is a perpetual curacy, value £160, in the patronage of the crown and bishop alternately. The parochial charities produce about £60 per annum, £36 of which are applied to educational purposes. The Baptists and Primitive Methodists have each a chapel, and there are schools for both sexes.*

The following three spooky tales all come from the Kingswood area of Bristol.

Two-Mile Hill

In the mid-1980s work at a garage in Two-Mile Hill in Kingswood used to be interrupted by a ghostly disturbance on a daily basis. Machines in the garage would spring to life – even with no power supplying them – and ghostly figures were seen walking through walls. Things got so bad that the area manager of the garage decided he would have to call in help to lay the spirit to rest.

The trouble began when a seventeenth-century cottage was sold after the death of its owner, Mr William Hucker, who had lived there for most of his life. It was later pulled down so flats could be built. It is thought that Mr Hucker haunts the garage and building because he did not want the cottage demolished.

The Kingswood area of Bristol early last century.

Kings Chase Shopping Centre, Regent Street

Some of the shops in the Kings Chase Shopping Centre in Bristol's Kingswood area were plagued by a poltergeist in August 1976.

Kettles boiled, eerie rustlings were heard, phantom footsteps walked the stairs, doors opened and slammed shut of their own accord and display stands were disturbed by invisible hands. A newsagent, a baker and a television retailer were all affected. Staff told the *Bristol Evening Post* of their experiences. Mrs May Owen, in the newsagents, claimed she had even heard the ghost speak. 'I was talking to a customer and we both happened to say "yes" at the same time, but we also distinctly heard a man's voice say "yes" behind us, but there was nobody there'.

Mrs Owen said a noise like the rustling of silk could be heard when the shop was quiet, and a heavy door leading to some stairs often opened and closed on its own. 'Our electric kettle has been switched off after we have had a cup of tea and then it suddenly turns itself on again and starts boiling,' she said. However, the strangest thing to happen was when a birthday card flew through the air. All the staff have at some point heard odd rattling noises and somebody, or something, moving about.

'It doesn't worry me working in the shop, but I've never experienced anything like it before,' Mrs Owen said at the time.

Next door, in the television shop, a man was heard climbing the stairs, and in the bakers an assistant heard a man walk up the stairs and use the toilet. When staff went to investigate they found the room empty.

The Kingswood complex is built on the exact site of the surgery where Dr E.M. Grace, the brother of the famous cricketing W.G. Grace, used to practice.

The Night Watchman: The Whiteley Tabernacle

Shortly before Christmas in 1928 an extraordinary incident was reported at the Whiteley Tabernacle in Chapel Road, Kingswood.

The annual Christmas bazaar was to be held on the Saturday and Mr J.B. Taylor had been asked to act as night watchman on the Friday night. While the organisers of the bazaar were waiting for him to turn up they were startled to hear three loud groans in the gallery of the hall. On searching the area, no one was found.

Mr Taylor, who was an elderly man, didn't arrive and so they locked up for the night. They later found out that Mr Taylor had collapsed and died at his home at precisely the same time that the groans had been heard.

The Whiteley Tabenacle in Hanham is where John Wesley, preaching at Hanham Mount, founded Methodism in 1739.

Another old view of the Kingswood area.

Arno's Manor Hotel, Brislington

When he became manager of the Parkside Hotel in May 1996, John Bird found he had to accommodate some unearthly sitting tenants.

Staff at the hotel claim to have witnessed a number of spectres over the years, and ghostly incidents reported at the hotel included:

- Phantom nuns walking the corridors, and figures wearing grey habits in guest rooms
- A door that rattled and shook whenever it was locked
- A ghostly maid in an old-fashioned uniform walking through a wall
- A basket of toiletries was flung through the air at a maid as she left a room after cleaning it

At the time, the most recent ghost to appear was that of an elderly man wearing a tweed suit. Rob Green, the bar manager, was cashing up after an evening's work when he caught sight of an old man in the reflection of the bar mirror – but when he turned around there was no one there. Mr Bird however was not too bothered by these spooky events and told the *Bristol Evening Post*: 'The ghosts have never hurt anybody. They're more like part of the family'.

One guest, however, who stayed at the hotel was so terrified by the sound of scratching and whispering in his room that he checked out of the hotel the next day.

In July 1996 John arranged for a team from the Cheltenham branch of the Student Parapsychological Society Research Group to investigate. As part of their investigation the team of ghost hunters spent an evening in the hotel, and found evidence of four different centres of paranormal activity.

The building was originally part of the Mount Pleasant complex built in around 1760 for William Reeve, a Quaker and wealthy copper smelter who had works at Crews Hole in Bristol. The architect was James Bridges, who had also built Bristol Bridge, Royal Fort and St Nicholas church in Bristol. The stables and servants quarters were built as a 'folly' in the style of a castle – these days they form The Black Castle pub (which features in the next story).

William Reeve used iridescent black slag blocks, a waste product of his copper works to assemble the buildings. At the time of its construction it was known locally as 'Black Slag Castle', however 'The Devil's Cathedral' was the inspirational name coined for it by Horace Walpole in 1766. Reeves went bankrupt in 1775 and died in 1778.

The original building also incorporated a unique bathhouse with an imposing gateway and colonnade frontage. The gateway niches were filled with statues saved from the famous Newgate and Lawfords Gate in Bristol, and some of the original statues are now preserved in the St Nicholas Church Museum in Bristol. The bath house was used in the 1900s as a showroom for antiques but by the late 1930s was standing empty. It became too dangerous to enter by the 1950s and was finally demolished.

Through the efforts of the Council for the Preservation of Ancient Bristol, Sir Clough William-Ellis accepted the Mount Pleasant Colonnade in 1957 for re-building among his architectural treasures at Portmerion, North Wales.

Today, the Parkside Hotel operates under the name Arno's Manor Hotel and is currently owned by Zoffany Hotels, part of the famous Forestdale Hotel Group. The chapel and staircase of the manor have been fully restored and the restaurant is set among the historic nun's cloisters.

The Black Castle, Brislington

The spirit of a child has been seen at The Black Castle pub in Brislington. A woman saw a little girl walk past her in the ladies' toilets and greeted the child with a friendly 'hello' – but the girl had inexplicably vanished.

The *other* resident spirit is altogether more complex and challenging, and has often been spotted at the top of the castle's highest tower. Stories have circulated for decades about the ghost of a nun, and some barstool pundits suggest she committed suicide rather than confess to an illicit pregnancy. Teresa and Bruce Boorer, who were the pub's assistant managers in 1992, have spoken of 'weird shadows that moved about', sightings that they associated with the nun.

Researching a book on Brislington ghosts in 1993 when The Black Castle was under new management, Ken Taylor was fortunate enough to enjoy a private tour of the whole building, including the chapel. 'Although dilapidated, the chapel was still beautiful,' he said, 'with stained glass windows and a vaulted ceiling of elegant white plaster studded with rosettes and swirls'.

Karen Kane, who then managed the pub along with husband Trevor, was Ken's guide and told him of her experiences of the ghost.

In the summer of 1992 a regular patron of the pub, a truck driver in his forties, was taken by candlelight to the chapel at around 10 p.m. In the chapel he laughed out loud in disbelief at the legend of the ghostly nun. At 6 a.m. the next morning, as he was starting his delivery run, he drove past The Black Castle and noticed the door atop the fire escape was open. At that exact moment the rear doors of his lorry flew open.

Believing there to be an intruder, the truck driver immediately called the police. It was only when they arrived and triggered the alarm system that the Kanes were alerted to the situation. No malfunction was found either with the door lock or the alarm system.

Owing to the unnerving nature of the events, the truck driver was again taken to the chapel in order to apologise for his disrespect. Things were quiet afterwards, however, shortly before the pub was closed for extensive refurbishment, Karen

The Black Castle.

watched an illuminated fire escape 'EXIT' sign flash on and off repeatedly (it had worked perfectly both before and after this incident), she understood the nun was saying goodbye.

In 2003 Ken spoke to assistant manager Miss Louise Noon, who assured him that the ghost was still very active. One night after work in August 2002, Louise, her mum and two locals were watching television in the main bar. She says that at around 1 a.m 'two glasses shot off a shelf and smashed'. The gathering soon dispersed.

The restaurant, which was until June 2003 situated across the courtyard from the main bar, became the main focus of paranormal activity. On numerous occasions Louise put down small items like pens, cutlery etc., only to find them gone moments later when she went to retrieve them. Mysterious chills were also often felt there. It reached the point where some of the staff became frightened of entering the restaurant at around midnight – when manifestations were at their most intense. Even Louise's cat, Tommy, had an aversion to the restaurant. Louise said: 'He would stop, stare and meow, but would not go in'.

Despite one report of 'headless nuns' being seen on the premises, Ken says he doubts that a nun would be responsible for this particular haunting. After all, the building has never been a convent and, although nuns are often associated with chapels, this one was privately built by a Quaker.

'Clearly though, the modern use of the building – which was frequented by the local Hell's Angels motorcycle chapter in the 1980s – would be incompatible with the presence of any peace-loving spirit. And that sort of emotional tension could be the cause of the poltergeist phenomena,' says Ken. 'The conflicting energies could be discharged in a series of startling events, like psychic earthquakes'.

The Black Castle's walls are studded with relics from bygone Bristol, each of which, according to the *Theory of Stone Recording*, could contribute its own psychic energy to the already heady atmosphere of this unique place. Not surprisingly, the chapel in the tower is not open to the public.

Betty's ghost, Siston Brook

The ghost of Betty Wilkins is said to haunt the area around Siston Brook, where she suffered a most painful death.

In 1788 Betty worked as a servant to the miller of Willsbridge. The area around the mill consisted of millpond, willow grounds and brook, with marshy fields on either side. It was definitely a brighter place in summer than in the bleak misty months of winter.

Betty's body was found floating in the millpond, washed up against the willows on Tuesday 13 September 1788. It was thought at first that she had drowned, but when her body was opened up and examined at an inquest on Thursday 25 September the actual cause of death given was arsenic poisoning.

When Mr Sherring, the Keynsham surgeon who carried out the post mortem, discovered that the girl was pregnant, the jury put two and two together and assumed a verdict of *felo de se* (self-murder suicide) carried out for reasons of fear and shame. Although a married woman, Betty had not had any contact with her husband for some time and the identity of her lover was either unknown or deliberately suppressed.

Betty's corpse was taken from the mill and buried at a crossroads. Suicide in the eighteenth century was classed as a crime committed by individuals in league with the Devil. Suicides were therefore buried at a crossroads, rather than in consecrated ground, and usually with a stake through the heart, to stop them from walking. Ideally, the wood used for the stake would be of elm or ash, the protective trees, and the stake served the same purpose as a cockerel on a weather vane – acting as a guard against evil from the four points of the compass.

It is not known for certain where Betty lies, however, a famous crossroads grave to the north of Poulton in Gloucestershire is called 'Betty's Grave' and possibly dates from the time of Wilkins' death. Wherever she was laid to rest, it would have been at a remote spot due to the very real fear of haunting. Perhaps we may never know.

A spooky Night at Ashton Court

Venturing out of the city a little to the south and west takes us to the Long Ashton area of Bristol, and Ashton Court. Genevra Jones from the *Bristol Evening Post* spoke to Olivier Verngault about his solitary vigil spent at the Court.

As a reporter for the *Bristol Evening Post*, Olivier Vergnault is used to taking a cool, calm view of events unfolding around him. He also thought ghost tales were just invented to frighten children and attract tourists. But when he was assigned the job of spending All Hallow's Eve alone in haunted Ashton Court – it was a different story.

Chris Wood, the estate manager, recounted the bloody history of the place and some of the spooky incidents he had experienced in twelve years of working on the estate. Olivier recalled: 'He talked of a headless horseman who rides the estate on moonlit nights, of ladies dressed in grey floating through locked doors and of footsteps heard at night. Chris told me of the ghostly black dogs which had terrified his own dog one night and of the uneasy sensation workers on the estate sometimes felt, as if someone – or something – was watching unseen'.

Chris told Olivier of an incident he experienced soon after moving to the estate. One night he heard one of the windows of the Clock Tower slam against the woodwork even though there wasn't the slightest breeze. The next day he nailed the window shut, but the following night the nails were pulled out and the window banged open once more. Again he had the window nailed shut and again it was forced open and slammed.

Ashton Court in the early 1900s.

The incident recurred regularly over three months. On the last occasion, the window had been secured with screws and ropes. But even those were forced open and once more the window smashed. Chris recalled: 'It stopped after that, as though the house had finally accepted me'.

This story made Olivier determined to spend his night in the Clock Tower. He said: 'I left the estate that day, smiling – not a believer.

'However, when I returned at midnight a week later armed with a sleeping bag, a thin mattress, warm clothes and my trusty torch, the smile was long gone'.

It faded still further when Chris greeted him with the most recent incident. A few days earlier Chris had been sitting at his desk at 3 p.m. when his chair was violently shaken, as if someone had grabbed it from behind and given it a serious push.

'I nearly fell off,' Chris told Olivier. 'I thought it was an earthquake so I ran downstairs, where a function was being held, to ask if everybody was all right'.

'They just looked at me like I was the village idiot. They hadn't felt anything at all'.

Full of trepidation Olivier climbed the treacherous spiral staircase to the Clock Room, laid down his mattress and set up camp.

He remembered: 'I attempted to sleep, torch in one hand and a small panic alarm button reassuringly close by. I curled up inside my sleeping bag, my back facing the dark hole, which served as a door.

'Although I did not believe any ghosts, spectre or ghouls would be coming to get me, I covered my face inside the sleeping bag, leaving only a small opening to breathe. If I did not believe, I certainly did not want to see either, but why bother covering your eyes when the sounds can be just as frightening?

'Within an hour of Chris's departure, the creaking noises started. I didn't worry too much at first because such creaks are normal in any old house. But soon I could hear footsteps in the neighbouring room. Then they grew louder. And closer. I was so tense I forgot to breathe. My imagination began to run riot.

'The steps grew louder still. What should I do? Leap from my sleeping bag to cuff the intruder around the head with a rolled-up copy of the *Bristol Evening Post* or stay put and hope whatever it was went away?

'The steps retreated, only to grow louder a few minutes later. It sounded like someone was pacing the corridor rather than climbing the stairs. Whatever it was still sounded too close for comfort.

'I hardly slept a wink after that. I was too terrified. The footsteps returned again during the small hours.

'Twice I thought about reaching for the panic button, but it lay outside the sleeping bag and I dared not make any noise for fear of attracting attention.

'Despite all that I must have dozed off, for the next thing I know a light was being shone in my face and a cup of coffee placed in my hand. "You all right there, mate?" asked a voice. It was 7.30 a.m. and the cleaner, who had been warned of my presence, had crept up to see if I had survived my ordeal.

'I didn't see any ghosts but hearing footsteps in the night was more than enough to convince me. As for returning to Ashton Court and spending another night on a ghost hunt, I don't think so. I'm still getting over the nightmares from my first visit'.

The manor of Ashton was clearly a wealthy estate, and can be traced back to the Domesday Book. Ashton Court mansion developed over the centuries from around 1390, when Thomas de Lyons married heiress Margaret Blanket. However, the purchase of the estate in 1545 by wealthy Bristol merchant John Smyth – Sheriff, Alderman, and twice Mayor of the city – is of particular historical significance, as it marked the beginning of an association that was to last four centuries. During this time the Smyth family (pronounced Smith) acquired extensive estates in and around the city of Bristol.

The Smyths lived in Corn Street and used Ashton Court to entertain fellow merchants. Then the family took up residence at Ashton Court and lived there until the 1700s, when they fell into debt and the house was bought by the family lawyer Jarrit Smith, who had married into the Smyth family. Jarrit Smith took over the house and changed the spelling of his name to Smyth. He was the first person to begin mining the Long Ashton coalfield. He also traded between the West Indies and Europe and became involved in the slave trade.

Bristol City Council acquired Ashton Court Estate in 1959 and after extensive repair works to the mansion a number of rooms were restored for public use, including a Visitor Centre and exhibition room in the old stables.

Chapter Four

On the Templars' Land

The Press Worker, Old Market

Journalists in Bristol not only write about ghosts, they sometimes share a building with them.

In August 1988, on the top floor of the *Western Daily Press* offices, used by Nat West bank, in Old Market, a ghost made its presence known.

Lights mysteriously switched themselves on and off, lifts were called to empty floors and stunned workers even saw a white-coated figure disappear through locked doors. On three occasions in a six-month period the apparition put in an appearance. On one occasion a petrified female employee ran screaming from a storeroom as the ghost passed by.

This ghost is not into making spooky noises, but likes to walk through fire doors and haunt the old photographic darkroom.

Graham Croker told the *Bristol Evening Post* in 1988 about the latest visit he had had from the spook. He was talking to colleague Norman Bushell on the fifth floor of the building when they both saw a figure heading toward the training room: 'I said, "The cleaner is not coming in tonight." And then we both saw the person walk straight through the locked door,' said Mr Croker.

Norman Bushell said if they had not gone to investigate and found the door locked he would have put money on it being the cleaner. 'There was not a soul there,' he said.

The Printers Devil, Old Market

The Printers Devil public house in Old Market has been the scene of plenty of poltergeist activity – including saucepans hurtling from the top of the kitchen fridge into the back yard.

Views of the Old Market area of Bristol in the early 1900s.

In December 1995, Nik Skorecki and Andy Payne went on a ghost hunt and spent the night in the cellars of the pub, which was used as a morgue in the eighteenth century. The cellar is undoubtedly a spooky sort of place – there's even a space hacked out of the rock for a coffin. But Andy didn't find it at all frightening: 'I'd have liked to have seen something and become a believer, but… well to be honest, the only thing that disturbed my slumber was the cellar's cooling fan,' he told the *Post*.

Despite lying only feet apart, Nik experienced a very different night: 'It was 7 a.m. and the night had been very quiet. Andy was asleep when I was astonished to see a huge figure – much larger than life – walk straight past us and through the door behind.

'The costume was from another age, perhaps 200 years or more ago. I didn't find it at all frightening. Then four black shadows swirled above my head before shooting off. The experience left me dumbfounded – it was two or three days before I got over it. But I also felt a tremendous sense of happiness afterwards,' he said.

Seeking Company in Temple Meads

In January 1978, twenty-seven-year-old Mrs Faye Mitchell-King took up a new post as a secretary with John Davidson's distribution company, providing pipes to the farming and housing industry.

Faye was completely unaware though that the warehouse where she was to work was the focus of a haunting by a short elderly grey-haired man. She only found out about the ghost when she asked her colleagues who the 'strange man who kept hanging around the warehouse' was. She told the *Bristol Evening Post* in 1978: 'I thought he was a customer. I was just going to the ladies when I saw this man of about sixty'.

Another secretary, Miss Lin D'Agostine, said at the time that a mirror, which was firmly stuck to the wall in the ladies' toilet, was mysteriously moved one day.

Mr George Morland was the managing director of Charles Cornish, the company that had occupied the warehouse in Temple Meads before John Davidson's. At the time, he tried to shed a little light on the mystery: 'A tramp died in the old property next door five or six years ago and his body remained there some time before anyone realised'.

Is it possible that the ghostly figure Faye saw was that of the vagrant? Perhaps he was looking for some company – especially after dying such a lonely death.

The Fire Station Haunting

The spirits of two Crusader knights and a monk have been seen since 1975 at the Fire Brigade headquarters on the Temple Back and Counter Slip area of Bristol.

An aerial view of the Temple Meads area in the last century.

Bristol Temple Meads train station, c. 1910.

On 29 October 1975, the *Bristol Evening Post* reported that the apparitions had been seen at least nine times. Mrs Iris Rhodes was a cook at the HQ at the time and claimed to have seen the ghost of the monk herself three times; 'I was standing counting my money, at about 8.30 p.m., when I saw someone standing by the pillar,' she said. 'As I went towards him, he disappeared'.

On another occasion she chased him downstairs with a glass of water. 'I thought someone was playing a practical joke on me, but he vanished,' she said. 'A person could not have got through the locked doors at the bottom of the stairs'.

Some of the firemen, who also claimed to have seen the ghostly monk, said he was wearing medieval dress, while the two crusading knights were described as having pointed hats. This would correspond with the dress of a member of the Knights Templar.

Frank Hollister, a leading fire control officer in 1975, told the *Bristol Evening Post* that he had seen two ghosts standing looking at him on the first landing of the stairs. 'I saw two crusader knights with pointed hats,' he said. 'I got the impression they were looking at me and I was the object of some sort of discussion. One minute they were there and the next minute they were gone.'

'Every time I go in the foyer, the hairs on the back of my neck stand on end,' said Mr Hollister. 'We got used to saying "Oh Fred's about," whenever it got cold. It sometimes feels as though a block of ice has been shoved up your jumper'.

He and another colleague also came across a figure they mistook for a fireman, but as Mr Hollister approached – it disappeared in front of their eyes.

The ghostly apparitions walked through doors; lowered the temperature in centrally heated rooms and vanished into thin air. They appeared only at night, to the control room and canteen staff in the foyer area on the corner of Counterslip and Temple Back.

On 18 December 1992, Lesley Turney of the *Bristol Evening Post* reported that not only were the hauntings still continuing at the HQ but the fire brigade had also acquired a phantom at its Avonmouth Station. Fire brigade spokesman Chris Palmer said at the time: 'The lads say there have been sightings of weird figures in the engine house and around the doors. We think the station is built on the site of an old gas-mask factory, which received a direct hit in a bombing raid in Second World War.

'There's an awful lot of interest in the ghosts. Officers have often stayed up all night looking out for them. But they come at unexpected times. More than one person has been frightened half to death after feeling a cold hand on his shoulder when locking up late at night'.

Back at Temple Back HQ the haunting continued. Fire fighters had heard strange noises and reported seeing ghostly forms on the stairs. Some of the fire fighters even staged spine-chilling vigils through the long hours of the night in the hope of contacting the spirits. But the apparitions only appeared when the fire officers least expected them. Two of these ghosts were said to haunt the corridors of the main fire station – and one of them in particular was seen many times. He was described as wearing a pointed helmet – as in the 1975 incidents – and is now thought to be the ghost of a man who lived nearly 1,000 years ago. The second one was rarely seen, but the men who worked in the control room said that they had often felt uneasy there.

It is known that the Knights Templar owned the land in Temple Back between 1140 and 1308, before they were arrested for heresy, blasphemy and unnatural acts and their land handed over to a rival order. The land on which the fire brigade headquarters was built was not only where the Knights Templar buried their dead but was also used as a burial ground during the plague.

CHAPTER FIVE

SUBURBAN
SPECTRES

The Stone Circles, Stanton Drew

The small village of Stanton Drew is home to some prehistoric stone circles that stand in the fields just beyond St Mary's church.

There are three stone circles at Stanton Drew, and the Great Circle is one of the largest in the country. The other two, one to the southeast and one to the southwest, are smaller. Not much is known about these great stones – or megaliths – and the patterns they make in the landscape remain mysterious. Folklore has it that the stones at Stanton Drew, sometimes called The Fiddlers and the Maids or The Wedding, are members of a wedding party. Legend has it that a couple were lured by the Devil to marry on the Sabbath and while celebrating on the Green the whole party was turned to stone.

In the garden of the village pub, the Druids Arms, is a group of three large stones called The Cove. To the north of the village, across the river Chew, is a standing stone called Hautville's Quoit. It is thought that Stanton Drew was once a place of great importance during the later Stone Age due to the alignment of some of these stones.

Mr G. Peek was landlord of the Druid's Arms in the late 1970s. He said at the time that the whole village 'has connections with spooks,' and the pub was no exception. He reported the following events:

- The bathroom door of the pub used to open and close on its own
- Crashes were heard in the middle of the night and when the Peeks went to investigate they found a large glass ashtray had shattered in the bar
- The rings on the electric stove turned themselves on
- Strange whining noises came at night from the stones called The Cove – just yards from the pub

The standing stones Stanton Drew today.

The pub used to be run by Bill Power's mother-in-law and one night when he was staying there he went downstairs into the bar. He saw what he described as 'a figure with long nails and a beard' coming in through the window. He picked up an alarm clock and threw it at the apparition, but it vanished and the clock smashed to pieces.

Mrs Ysobel Hawthorne and her husband Colonel Jack Hawthorne moved into The Manor at Stanton Drew in the early 1960s. The Manor was originally a fortified, L-shaped farmhouse, which had been rebuilt in 1756. 'There's hardly anyone living in an old house around here which hasn't got some sort of spirit or other,' Mrs Hawthorne said at the time.

When the Hawthornes first moved into the property they noticed an unpleasant feel about the place and a peculiar smell. Not long after, they found that objects kept smashing much too often to be mere accidents.

After the couple had the house fumigated to remove the unpleasant smell, the spirit became much less destructive. 'Rows of cups hanging in the kitchen would move about as if a child was running his hands along the shelf,' said Mrs Hawthorne.

They named the poltergeist 'George' and found that he also played with the heavy irons that hung in the grate of the front sitting room.

'We got the impression that George used to play up the back stairs in the house. My daughter said that a couple of the steps were warm to her feet and that George had been there,' she said. Mrs Hawthorne even heard George speak once in a 'nice Somerset voice' which sounded like that of a young boy of about ten or eleven years old. She was in the kitchen and spilt some melted dripping in her lap. George then said to her: 'Thee bin silly'.

In the late 1970s Ian Girvan was busy researching a book he was writing with Margaret Royal called *Bristol Ghosts and their Neighbours*.

In March 1977 he paid a visit to Mrs Linton who lived at The Cottage, and heard for himself some mysterious footsteps walking across the room above. Mrs Linton said the footsteps were a feature of The Cottage and she had got used to living with them. She recalled a time in 1972 when the stair carpet was removed so that the wood could be repainted. For the ten days that the stairs were bare she heard the footsteps even more clearly. 'I'm not the least bit frightened,' she declared. 'I should love to see it'.

However, she also told Ian of a far more dramatic experience. Not long after she first moved in to the house she had heard footsteps coming up the stairs toward her bedroom. Her dachshund dog ran to the door barking furiously, its fur standing on end. When she opened the door something rushed right across the room at an angle and the dog went after it. Nothing was caught.

Visitors to The Cottage have also witnessed strange things. A group of bell-ringers were with Mrs Linton in the front room when there was a great crash on the front door. When it was opened there was nobody there. Music seems to excite the ghost

The Druid's Arms, Stanton Drew.

of The Cottage. One evening when Mrs Linton was playing a recording of Mahler's *10th Symphony* the footsteps could be heard running around the room.

Sometime in the 1950s Mrs Linton discovered another room directly beneath the living room of The Cottage. Workmen were installing a boiler in the house when they found the room, the same size as the living room above it. The room was sealed up and no one has ever seen what, if anything, it contained. The only clues were some handmade green glass triangles found by the workmen.

The deeds to The Cottage in the village date back to 1614 but it was in existence long before that. A monastery at Stanton Drew had been destroyed by Henry VIII, and the young monks lodged in The Cottage – using the drawing room as a chapel.

An underground passage is another peculiar feature of Stanton Drew village. It can no longer be entered as it was sealed up for reasons of safety, however it is known to be about a third of a mile long and six feet high. It runs from Stanton Drew Church to Vicarage Farm and passes under the garden of The Cottage.

In 2004 the Ancient Monuments Laboratory of English Heritage carried out a magnetometer survey of the large field containing the Great Circle and the north-east circle. The results were astonishing and demonstrated that the megalithic remains are but the ruin of a much more important site than previously thought. Lying underneath the pasture within the Great Circle are the remains of a highly elaborate pattern of buried pits. The Great Circle itself is contained within a very large buried enclosure ditch – a well-known feature of later Neolithic Britain.

The Cove, which stand behind the Druid's Arms.

The Submerged Village, Chew Valley Lake

The area around Chew Stoke has changed very little since 1956. It is hard to imagine now, when looking at the vast lake built by Bristol Water Plc., that a village with farms, churches, mills and houses once stood in this place. The village was called Moreton.

Catherine Brown once lived in Moreton with her mother. One afternoon a very worried Elizabeth Brown reported her daughter missing to the police, and a major search was launched while the girl's mother waited anxiously at home in the hope that her daughter would turn up.

Many hours passed and then, as Elizabeth stood at the front door of the house, she gasped a sigh of relief to see Catherine suddenly coming toward her up the garden path. The girl, however, walked right past her mother and went up into her bedroom. Elizabeth could hear her daughter moving about upstairs, but hours later she discovered Catherine was no longer there.

The next day Catherine was found drowned near Stratford Mill in the village – she had been dead for at least twenty-four hours. It's almost as though Catherine didn't realise she had died, and had gone home as planned.

Since then there have been various sightings of the 'Ghost of Chew Valley Lake' – the most recent was reported in the *Bristol Evening Post* on 9 September 1999.

Three sightings were reported on the same night, which is now believed to be the anniversary of the girl's death. The ghost was described as being slightly built, wearing a white dress and heavy black lace-up boots from the Victorian era.

The closest encounter involved Blagdon man Chris Pugh, his daughter Sam and partner Wendy Gunning, who almost ran into the shadowy woman. They were driving home one night from the Chew Stoke direction when they encountered a woman crossing the road. She was wearing a three-quarter-length gown with a linen cape-style dress and hood and had long wavy hair. Chris said: 'I missed her by about four foot. I had my main beam headlights on and got no reaction from the ghost, even though I flashed the lights on her'.

The next report came from three young girls on their way home from a party in 1999. Marie and Louise Stuckey, who lived in Nempnett Thrubwell, and their friend Nicola Court, from Compton Martin, were travelling home with Nicola's parents when they spotted the woman. Marie told the *Bristol Evening Post*: 'She was solid but greyish and misty and was walking along the verge on the left by the old council yard by Kingshill Lane. She was wearing a mid-calf Victorian style dress and hobnail boots. Her hair was long and she was walking along with her hands behind her back'.

In the same report Carol Gillen, a hairdresser from Ubley, described her experience. Carol was going home in the same direction as the three girls when she saw the Chew Valley ghost: 'She was very solid and crossing the road to the lane opposite the bed and breakfast sign', Carol said. 'She wore a heavily embroidered Victorian

Chew Valley Lake.

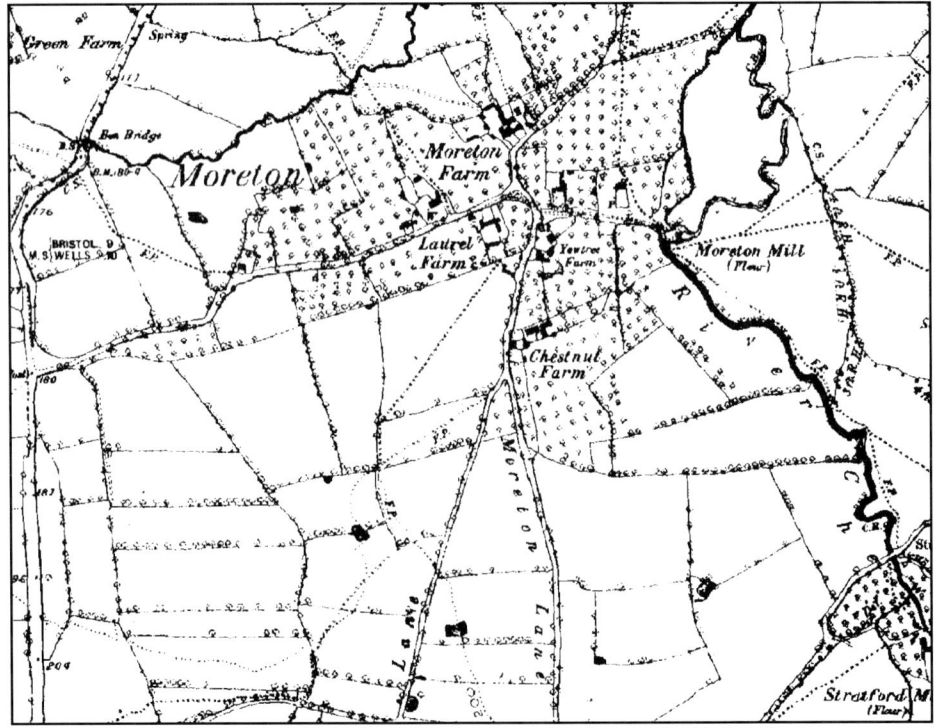

Map of Moreton village in the late nineteenth century.

style dress with leg-of-mutton sleeves, which were very full to the elbows. They were billowing back with the breeze. The whiteness of her dress was very bright, as if electric. Her hair was loose, thick, longish to the top of her shoulders and blowing off her neck'.

Carol said the woman walked with a strong and confident stride as if she knew where she was heading. She added: 'I thought at the time how stupid to be walking at this time of night as she had no torch, no coat and nothing on her head. Afterwards I realised it must have been a ghost as she took no notice of me at all'.

Stratford Mill, where Catherine's body was found, has since been rebuilt at the Blaise Castle Estate in Bristol.

A Ghostly Walker on the A38, Barrow Gurney

Drivers need to pay extra attention on the stretch of the A38 near the reservoir at Barrow Gurney.

A number of motorists over the years have been forced to swerve, or brake suddenly, to avoid a woman in a white coat who suddenly appears in front of them, crossing the road.

One young driver was horrified by the sudden appearance of this apparition. Believing her to be a real person he slammed on his brakes violently, skidded, but was able to stop safely. When he got out of the car there was no sign of the woman, but he noticed several skid marks made by other motorists at the same stretch of road.

Another man reported a similar experience. He was driving quite slowly behind a bus, and so was able to stop easily when the spectre stepped out in front of him. But again the woman in the white coat had vanished by the time he got out of the car.

A Request to be Laid to Rest

Henry Martin Gibbs was the squire of Barrow Court, Barrow Gurney. He was born on 30 May 1850, and he died on 22 April 1928. The story of his ghostly encounter has been passed down the generations. One version – as he told it to a villager during his lifetime – appeared in the Bristol *Evening Post* on 21 October 1967.

One evening, the story goes, Henry was standing at the front door looking down the drive when he saw in the dusk the figure of a woman glide across the grass in front of the old cedar tree.

'At first I thought it was one of the maids taking an evening stroll but noticed that she was somewhat peculiarly dressed,' said the squire. The figure wore a very long gown with a high ruffled collar.

'As I watched her she seemed to vanish into the wall which divided the court grounds from the churchyard.

'I went over to the place where I thought she had disappeared and marked it with a stone. The next day I got one of the masons to take that part of the wall down, and as he was digging out the foundations his spade hit something with a metallic ring. With some difficulty he unearthed a small metal box about eighteen inches square. When it was opened it was found to contain the skull of a woman'. The squire had the skull buried in the churchyard and the ghost was never seen again.

Barrow Gurney lies five miles to the west of Bristol. A Benedictine nunnery was established here around the beginning of the thirteenth century by one of the Fitz-Hardinges, to whom the manor belonged at the time. Henry VIII granted the manor to John Drew, of Bristol, who converted it into a private mansion. The house is now called Barrow Court, and was the seat of the Gores, in whose family it belonged between 1659 until 1855. Henry Gibbs purchased Barrow Court in 1884 when he became Lord of the Manor of Barrow Gurney. Henry also held the office of High Sheriff of Somerset in 1897 and the office of JP for Somerset.

If you are interested, more can be found out about the Gibbs and Gore families, and documents relating to Barrow Court on the Historical Manuscripts Commission website www.hmc.gov.uk.

Barrow Court, Barrow Gurney.

Brockley Court and Brockley Combe

There should really be a regular census carried out on the ghosts 'living' in Bristol. Brockley Combe, for instance, has been called the 'Most Haunted Spot in the West' with at least seven spooks:

Number one

Nobody is quite sure if the Bounding Ghost of Brockley Combe is male or female but a tall, thin form has been spotted bounding along the road through Brockley Combe before disappearing into a high hedge.

Number two

On the stroke of midnight every Christmas Eve it is said that a passengerless coach driven by a coachman dressed in eighteenth-century clothes drives down a ruined carriageway on the right-hand side of the Combe.

An antiquarian wrote in a local journal in 1922 that villagers who had seen the apparition said the coach made no noise as it approached, even though the coachman could be seen to be cracking his whip. Then the vision would vanish as quickly as it had appeared.

Number three

The best-authenticated ghost to haunt Brockley Combe is that of Dinah Swan, a ninety-year-old woman whose body was found outside a cottage at the foot of the Combe in December 1833. Dinah had dragged herself as far as the heavy iron gates of the big house nearby before falling dead from fright. The verdict at Dinah Swan's inquest was that she was 'found dead, supposed to have been frightened to death by some person or persons unknown'. She is said to haunt the Combe in the early hours of the morning.

Number four

John Bennet wrote in the *Bristol Evening World* in 1947 of a ghost seen on separate occasions by two women from Weston-super-Mare. Both had seen the figure of a man standing beneath a tree halfway up the Combe where the road forked. He was described as 'standing away from the trees and dressed in black with a white blob in front that looked like a large white collar'.

Number five

The ghost of an old woman is said to appear once every twenty-six years, and is said to bring madness and death to anyone who sees her. The last appearance was due in 1990, although no one claimed to have seen the ghost, and the next will be in 2016. The ghost was also due to appear in 1834 – maybe she put in an early appearance and frightened Dinah Swan to death?

Number six

The eleventh-century church of St Nicholas in Brockley is said to be haunted by 'mysterious footsteps, whisperings in the dark and the apparition of a little brown lady'.

Several people claim to have seen the little brown lady either cleaning the vestry or trotting along the aisle and up to the altar, reported *The Evening World* in 1947. One night a novelist ghost hunter and a psychic research investigator spent an all-night vigil in the church. They made a thorough examination of the church, locked and sealed all the doors and then settled down to wait. 'We did not see the woman in brown,' one of the investigators told the *Evening World*, 'but we did hear footsteps and strange whispering'.

St Nicholas church.

Another view of St Nicholas church, Brockley.

Finally at number seven – unless you know otherwise?

Sir Arthur Conan Doyle, Sir Ernest Bennett, Lord Curzon and the well-known ghost hunter Elliott O'Donnell all investigated the rumoured haunting of Brockley Court, where a hooded monk is supposed to roam.

Mr O'Donnell spent eight nights at Brockley Court and wrote: 'Only on one occasion did anything exciting happen. I was with several other men and one of them was very badly frightened. I have always believed he saw something superphysical, as his description of the thing that scared him tallied exactly with the phenomenon that the son of the then owner of the house told me he had seen on several occasions, and which led to the vacancy of the house. It was nothing like the monkish-looking thing Palmer faked'.

O'Donnell was referring to Mr Palmer who had been a student at Bristol University. His supposedly 'authentic' photograph of the ghostly monk in the house had gained a lot of publicity at the time but was later proved to be a fake.

Sir Arthur Conan Doyle's son, Adrian, shed a little light on the mystery in a letter to the *Western Daily Press* in February 1945. He said that Palmer had admitted to impersonating the ghost but that the real ghost had appeared immediately afterwards. Adrian said Palmer had written to his father: 'After I saw and felt the power of the real ghost in the haunted room I could not have posed again'.

Brockley Hall in its heyday.

Adrian Conan Doyle wrote, 'My father gives the incident in full in his book *Our African Winter*, and adds 'Most people will agree that it was a pity he posed at all and that it is deplorable that the work of honest men should be complicated by irresponsible buffoonery. It confirms what I have often said, that it is the researcher and the spectator who have to be watched and checked quite as much as the medium'.

The New Inn, Backwell

Just a mile or so away from Brockley Combe is the village of Backwell and a 200-year-old haunted pub.

When Jim Tonkin and his wife took over the running of The New Inn, on West Town Road, in the late 1960s, they found that the inn had more than just liquid spirits behind the bar.

Disembodied footsteps were heard on the stairs, a ghostly stranger suddenly appeared at the bar one night, obviously waiting to be served, and in the same room another non-existent customer touched a woman on the neck. On another occasion Mr Tonkin's spectacles disappeared from the bar counter of the pub and reappeared in the skittle alley. This spirit even took to levitating objects and on one occasion the 'pineapple' top of an ice bucket was gently wafted across the room.

A photograph of the New Inn, taken in the last century.

The New Inn today.

The Bowl Inn, Lower Almondsbury

Elizabeth Maronne is said to haunt both the Bowl Inn pub and the village of Lower Almondsbury. Inside the church of St Mary the Virgin is a memorial plaque that reads:

> *Beneath this place lye the bodies of John & Elizabeth Maronne in the memory of whom their father*
> *caus'd this monument to be put up. Elizabeth died in 1708 aged 6 John died in 1711 aged 5 their*
> *father a poore man born in the province of Dophine in the Kingdom of France he belevs that his sins*
> *were the cause that God took the life of his children.*

It is uncertain if Elizabeth and John were born in France or in England, but it is certainly very sad that both the children died so young. What sins did the father commit that could lead him to believe that God took his children away? According to the pamphlet produced by St Marys' Almondsbury Parochial Church Council, the children's father, John Maronne, who also died in 1711, believed God took his children as a punishment for him loving them too much.

Ghostly activity includes the sound of a child reciting nursery rhymes – heard both in the village and the Bowl Inn – and the sound of a child crying, when no child has been in the vicinity.

Elizabeth Maronne is just one of the ghosts that are reputed to haunt The Bowl Inn. The pub is also said to be home to two other ghosts – both women – whose

The inscription on the wall of the church of St Mary the Virgin.

The Bowl Inn today.

identity is unknown. One recent account comes from a man working at the Inn. He was in the dining area when out of the corner of his eye he saw a woman dressed in old-fashioned clothes walk towards the kitchen. She opened the swing doors and went through into the kitchen. The man immediately followed as he wasn't sure who she was but when he reached the kitchen there was no sign of anyone.

Another chilling account concerns another worker at the inn. He was busy painting the window frame in a bedroom upstairs when all of a sudden the air turned icy cold and he had the feeling that someone was watching him. But when he turned around there was no one there. The experience shook him up so much that he would not return to finish the job.

At the time of the 1881 census the owner and licensee of the Bowl Inn had been Fannie (Francis) Williams (née Martin), who lived at the inn with her two nephews. She was thirty-nine years old and a widow. Could Fannie be the ghostly apparition seen by the worker at the inn?

The Bowl dates back to 1146 when parts of the whitewashed stone inn were originally three separate cottages built to house the monks who were building the church of St Mary the Virgin next door.

Underground tunnels, built to offer protection against foreign invaders, ran beneath the cottages, the church and the priory (which is now a farmhouse).

The Bowl became a licensed inn in 1550 and was also used by James II sheriffs during the later part of the seventeenth century to try supporters of the Duke of Monmouth.

Almondsbury lies seven miles north of Bristol and is steeped in history. References can be traced back centuries to its appearance in Saxon charters and it is also mentioned in the Domesday Book of 1086. The village derives its name from one Aethelmund (or Ealhmund of Alomund), a Saxon village chieftain. The location provided an excellent defensive site and signs of entrenchment are still visible. So it's hardly surprising that ghostly activity has been recorded in this area.

The Bowl Inn was also the place where the infamous 'Princess Caraboo' arrived on 3 April 1817, and duped the people of the area – including many 'high society' elite – into believing she was a princess from a foreign land who spoke an unrecognisable language. In reality she was Mary Baker, the daughter of a cobbler, who lived in Witheridge, Devonshire. Until her deception was exposed the 'Princess' lived for a number of weeks at Knole Park – the home of Samuel Worrall, the Magistrate of the County.

The White Lady of Over Court, Almondsbury

The problem with most ghost stories is that spirits are usually seen by just one person at a time, which makes it difficult to corroborate a sighting. But just occasionally a spirit will appear to a group of people.

One of the strangest mass hauntings happened one winter evening in 1937. It was Friday 17 December when The White Lady of Over Court appeared to a dozen members of the East Compton Prize Band and turned an evening of carol playing into a nightmare.

The musicians had visited the court, a gabled Elizabethan mansion near Almondsbury, for years and were all well aware of the legend of the White Lady of Over Court. But as they scrunched up the drive a little after 7 p.m. any talk of ghosts was strictly light-hearted. Minutes later they all staggered away convinced that they had witnessed an apparition. Perhaps the spirit didn't like the idea that she wasn't being taken seriously?

John Purnell, aged fourteen at the time, was a veteran of half a dozen previous visits but on this occasion he believed he encountered two ghosts. Since that fateful night he believes he has learned the truth about one of them.

John and his fellow carollers were halfway through the second verse of *Hark, The Herald Angels Sing*, when John, who was on the outer edge of the group glanced along the building.

In an article published in the *Bristol Evening Post* on 24 December 1988, he recounted his tale: 'At the left-hand corner was a tree,' he recalled, 'and I became aware of a figure standing at the side of it – very tall, white but not shining and with a shape I could not describe. It disappeared, and then reappeared before finally vanishing. I waited to see the reaction of my companions, but nobody mentioned it, and I knew that if I'd said I had seen the White Lady they would have treated it as a huge joke. The best thing to do was keep quiet.

'We completed our carols and trudged back through the entrance arch – until I suddenly realised that everybody had stopped. In the tangle of the undergrowth, the full moon was throwing odd shadows – but it could not obscure the fact that there was a bright white figure less than the length of a cricket pitch away'.

Another account tells of the band's lantern going out just before the sighting. One of the younger members of the group shouted: 'Look there, through the gap', and the figure of the White Lady could be seen floating just above the ground with a distinctive bluish glow radiating from it.

'It was about the size of an average person with a tall, pointed head-dress, and it moved in a zigzag manner away from us,' John recalled. 'It appeared to go behind trees and through a hedge as we watched. Moving further away it became smaller, until it finally disappeared. I suppose the episode lasted about thirty seconds. For several moments nobody moved until someone broke the spell with: "Well, I'll be damned".

'Keeping a little closer together, we continued our carols at a few small cottages. A local farmer stopped his car and shouted: "What's the matter with the band tonight?"

'We've seen the White Lady', we choroused.

'Aye, it sounds like it", he replied, driving off in gales of laughter.'

John continued: 'This was the first time a whole group of people had seen the phantom; the local papers reported it, there was a lot of talk at the time, and then it passed into local folklore'.

And what of the ghost that appeared only to fourteen-year-old John Purnell before the White Lady made her appearance?

'I was watching a television programme about deer a couple of years ago,' he said. 'It showed how, in winter, they will stand on their hind legs to strip trees for food. Something clicked. It was exactly the shape I had seen at the side of Over Court all those years ago. There had been white deer on the estate, so my private phantom was well and truly laid to rest. As for the one we all saw, though – I'm still watching television, but I've seen nothing like it yet'.

The White Lady is thought to be the wife of an early owner of Over Court, shot or stabbed by her husband for having an affair with a member of a prominent local family. She is said to have staggered wounded from the house to the fishpond at the bottom of the garden and drowned – and it is from here that she is believed to rise and stalk the grounds.

When she was seen by the East Compton Prize Band members she was heading directly for the pond – through undergrowth so thick that when some of the braver young lads went back to the scene a couple of days later they found it impossible to penetrate.

Over Court lies two miles south west of Almondsbury, and was built around the same time as Knole park on the site of a fourteenth-century house. Although the court was demolished after a fire in the early 1980s and modern housing now stand on the site, the distinctive clock tower remains. One of the former occupants was Bristol's most important slave-trader Sir James Laroche who purchased Over Court sometime around the mid-1700s. Laroche had at least two African servants who lived with him at Over Court; James Long (died 17 March 1773) and Charles Morson (died 16 February 1776).

CHAPTER SIX

LIVING WITH SPIRITS

THE RICHARD HOPE-HAWKINS STORY

If you think you may have some psychic ability lying dormant then Bristol is certainly the place to awaken it, as the following story shows.

Theatre director Richard Hope-Hawkins, from Clifton, recalls some of his strange experiences:

'The first sort of psychic experience I had in Bristol happened when I was about eleven. My Godmother's husband bought a house in Pembroke Road.

'It was being stripped out ready to convert and I remember going to look at it with a dog called Sweep who was from our family farm.

'The dog wouldn't go in the house at all. I managed to get him into the hallway and his heckles literally rose and I had to tie him outside by the entrance. And I had a very uneasy feeling; it was the first time I had really sensed anything. I sensed, almost sorrow.

'I couldn't understand it and I cut the visit short. I had wanted to look around the house but was only in it for a matter of minutes. When I came outside the dog had run off leaving just the collar and lead dangling on the post. Sweep didn't return home for two or three days'.

Richard's next experience came about a year later when poltergeist-type activity began one night when he was alone in the family home at No. 71 Linden Road. Richard had gone to bed about 8.30 p.m. when a stone hit his window, then another and another. A whole host of stones then showered inexplicably on to his bedroom window and the conservatory, breaking one of the windows.

This went on for about five weeks. Richard said: 'It got to the stage where the police were called. They thought someone had been using a catapult, but one policeman was taken off the case because he said he had seen a stone rise from the garden and hurled up towards the house. My parents said that he was sent away almost in disgrace.

Richard Hope-Hawkins.

'Most of the activity took place at the back of the house. I remember my uncle coming into my bedroom wearing a World War Two tin helmet, because we were all frightened of being hit by flying glass. I think in all, between fifteen and twenty windows were broken during the whole period and it only stopped when I was sent away for a few days. When I came back to the house nothing else ever happened there again'.

Richard shared some supernatural experiences with his close friend Alex Schlesinger, who lived in St Ronan's Avenue, Redland. 'When I was fourteen I remember we were listening to music in Alex's living room and I saw what I thought was a woman, materialise, glide across the room and de-materialise. I said nothing for half a minute and then I said, "Alex, did you see that?" and he said, "Oh yes, don't be silly, we see it all the time"'.

In around 1970 the two men visited a large Georgian house with stables, outhouses and greenhouses, over the Clifton Suspension Bridge on the Smythe estate.

'A London property developer had bought the house and was going to pull it down. Alex had met the owner as a schoolboy and he had got permission from the

London property owner to take whatever he wanted and explore the house and the grounds.

'The key had been left for us under a stone by the front door, but the big double iron gates were padlocked, so we had to climb over a wall. Once we had got into the house we wandered around for probably an hour. We went into every room, and picked up some bits and pieces that Alex was going to take with him.

'When we came out of the house we saw an elderly couple and a car in front of us. We couldn't understand this, as we hadn't heard a car coming up the gravel driveway.

'The elderly woman was white haired and looked a bit like Miss Haversham from *Great Expectations* and the man was tall and slightly bent. We started talking to the couple and they said that they were the servants of the house. The man was the one doing the talking, I remember he said, "We opened the…" and Alex said "The door", finishing his sentence for him. He had to be prompted as if he'd had a stroke or something. We spoke to the couple for about five minutes and then Alex said that we were just going to wander around. We both felt a bit uneasy, something wasn't quite right.

'We got to the side of the house and I looked up to see a face against the window. I said to Alex "There's somebody looking out of the window in the servant's quarters upstairs". Alex looked up and said "Oh my God". We both knew there was no one else in the house and we both ran to the front of the house. There was no car and no people; we hadn't heard a car approach or leave. We ran like hell, and when we jumped over that wall the sunshine hit us and we could hear birds singing – at that point we realised that while we were talking to the old couple, it had been very deathly quiet'.

For many years Richard was a great friend of Bristol-born pianist Russ Conway who sadly died after a long battle with cancer:

'A few days after Russ's death, I had a phone call from composer Les Read, who asked me, "Do you believe in the afterlife?" and I replied, "Yes".

'He said, "Have you heard of Betty Shires?" and I said, "She's a very famous medium". He said, "Yes, she's had a message. Actually she's a bit annoyed as she keeps getting woken up in the middle of the night – it's Russ!"'

'I told him that I'd always been led to believe that when you passed away it takes some time for the spirit to settle and any contact to be made on this side. However Les said, "Well no, he's composing, he's bombarding her with things"'.

'More than 1,500 people attended Russ's funeral service. Les gave me a lift to the reception afterwards and he handed me some letters that had been dictated to Betty Shires with references to me in'.

'Betty had asked, "Who's Richard, connected with Russ?"'

'Les replied, "A very good friend of Russ's". She said, "Well I have a message for Richard"'.

'Russ had spoken through Betty saying, "I am going to keep an eye on you Richard, I want things to go well for you"'.

'And the words he said, which convinced me that it could only have been Russ, were, "I am going to keep an eye on you from this Eagle's Nest viewpoint"'.

'Not an unusual thing to say perhaps, but Russ and I had shared an interest in pre-World War Two German history. When he was alive, Russ and I had agreed that we'd like to visit parts of Germany and Auschwitz, and in particular we'd love to go to Berchtesgaden and take tea in Hitler's retreat which was high up the mountains, you drove up a long winding road – it was of course called The Eagle's Nest'.

'We never talked about it much because we thought people might think we were a bit right wing, which was far from the truth. So for Betty Shires, one of the most famous mediums in the world, to get a message from Russ saying the words "Eagle's Nest viewpoint" clinched it for me'.

CHAPTER SEVEN

OVER TO YOU

As promised earlier in the book, here is a short selection of ghostly reports from Bristol that require further investigation. If you fancy a spot of ghost hunting then these are some suggested starting places, or if you know anything about these spooks I will be happy to hear from you.

Parry's Ghost

Stoke Bishop and Combe Dingle seem to have been especially haunted in Victorian times. Parry's Lane is named after a well that once stood near the top of a hill approaching the Downs. It was here that a man named Parry committed suicide by slitting his own throat. His ghost has been seen sitting beside the well.

Yatton church

In February 1952, a parish warden told the *Bristol Observer* that he had heard footsteps in Yatton church when it was empty, and had then seen a grey-robed lady moving about around the tombs of medieval knights. Others have apparently also seen the figure on different occasions, including the former church organist who claimed to have seen the grey-robed lady move slowly across the aisles on no less than three separate occasions.

The Phantom Horse, Stapleton

If you walk along the lane that runs along the back of Stapleton church in the direction of Blackberry Hill you will see a gate on the right leading in to a field. In this field the ghost of a white horse has been seen on many occasions over many years.

The Hanging Man

In Stapleton woods the body of a man is sometimes seen hanging from a rope tied to the branch of a tree. As the startled witness approaches, he vanishes.

The White Horse, Stoke Bishop/Shirehampton

The River Trym flows from Henbury through Combe Dingle to the Avon, through an uninhabited wooded region between Stoke Bishop and Shirehampton.

Flooding was frequent and when a travelling showman allowed his horse to graze on the riverbank it became stuck in the mud. The place was so remote that no help was available and the poor beast died of exposure and starvation. When mist hangs over the valley the ghost of a white horse is said to appear.

Royal York Crescent, Clifton

Royal York Crescent in Clifton is said to be haunted by the ghost of a woman described as a 'blue nun'.

Loyal Sally, Hanham Farm

An ancient farmhouse at Hanham is known locally as 'Sally on the Barn'. Sally was a serving girl during the Civil War who is said to have been killed by the Roundheads when she refused to give information as to the whereabouts of some Cavaliers. It is believed that she was killed trying to escape through the trap door on to the barn roof, as this is where her ghost is seen.

Hope Chapel Hill

The ghost of a beautiful woman in eighteenth-century dress has been seen on Hope Chapel Hill and near the chapel itself.

Whitchurch

The ghost of a German Air Force officer has been seen at what was Whitchurch Aerodrome by a cleaner and various other personnel.

Saltford

An old manor house at Saltford has been graced with the presence of an elderly lady who would appear in a rocking chair.

Somerdale

A Roman soldier is said to haunt the Fry's chocolate factory in Somerdale. One employee claims to have seen the ghost on three separate occasions and, on further research, has discovered that the factory is built on part of a Roman settlement.

Troopers Hill, St Anne's

The sound of ghostly partying – bottles clinking, shouts of laughter and loud voices – has been heard on Troopers Hill, but in keeping with the unexplained of Bristol there are no physical bodies for the sounds to emanate. According to local legend the Roundheads are to blame for the noise. Historically it is thought that the Roundheads were a very grim and sober bunch, but these ghosts must have something to celebrate.

Other titles published by Tempus

Haunted Gloucester

EILEEN FRY AND ROSEMARY HARVEY

From paranormal manifestations at Gloucester Docks to the ghostly activity of a monk who is said to haunt the city's twelfth-century Cathedral, this spine-tingling collection of supernatural tales recalls strange and spooky happenings in the city's ancient streets, churches, theatres and public houses, including The Kingsholm Inn and Bridge Inn. Here's a glimpse into the ghostly legacy of Gloucester's past.

0 7524 3312 1

Bristol Times *revisited*

DAVID HARRISON

This book is a collection of some of the articles drawn from the first year of the Bristol Times Supplement of the Bristol Evening Post. Each extract recalls an aspect of the city's lively, and sometimes turbulent, history. From tales of fairs, workhouses, riots and gaols, to accounts of star appearances at the hippodrome and the success of Fry's chocolate factory, each piece provides an insight into Bristol's past.

0 7524 2844 6

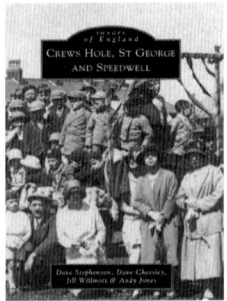

Crews Hole, St George and Speedwell

DAVE STEPHENSON, DAVE CHEESLEY, JILL WILLMOTT AND ANDY JONES

Illustrated with over 200 archive pictures, this collection evocatively captures the histories of Netham, Crews Hole, St George and Speedwell in east Bristol. Snapshots of everyday life combine with vistas of the industries upon which these communities relied, particularly the collieries and chemical works whose chimneys towered over this area of the city. This fascinating volume shows the great changes which have taken place in commerce, heavy industry, transport and residential areas.

0 7524 2948 5

Filton Voices

Jane Tozer and Jackie Sims

This book brings together the personal memories of people who lived and worked in Filton from the 1930s, vividly recalling the farms and fields before they were lost to housing. The voices tell of childhood games, the close-knit community, shops and entertainment, as well as the devastating effects of bombing raids on the aircraft factory, cheek by jowl with the village. The stories are complemented by a hundred photographs drawn from the private collections of the contributors.

0 7524 3097 1

If you are interested in purchasing other books published by Tempus, or in case you have difficulty finding any Tempus books in your local bookshop, you can also place orders directly through our website

www.tempus-publishing.com